NEW HORIZONS FOR COLLEGE WOMEN

NEW HORIZONS FOR COLLEGE WOMEN

EDITED BY LEO C. MULLER AND OUIDA G. MULLER

KATE HEVNER MUELLER

FRANK A. ROSE

SEYMOUR A. SMITH

GRELLET C. SIMPSON

EDNA P. AMIDON

ANNA L. ROSE HAWKES

MARGUERITE W. ZAPOLEON

ANNE ROE

HAROLD TAYLOR

LEO C. AND OUIDA G. MULLER

FOREWORD BY ERNEST V. HOLLIS

Public Affairs Press, Washington, D. C.

TO

DR. CHARLES PINCKNEY HOGARTH

For his outstanding leadership in higher education

FOREWORD

My interest in the education of women has been an abiding concern. For this reason I enjoyed and found it professionally profitable to read each of the outstanding manuscripts presented by some of the nation's most distinguished educators and leaders.

This volume has been prepared to share some of the sense and flavor of a formal symposium on The Education of Women which, most appropriately, was held during the 75th anniversary celebration of the Mississippi State College for Women. It is not easy to recreate the intellectual and emotional climate developed by a series of formal papers and informal sessions. Nevertheless, the editors have done a most refreshing job in making you feel you were there.

In commending this book to you for thoughtful reading and the incorporation of relevant ideas into your own philosophy, there is no intention of implying that I endorse all of each paper. The views of the authors nevertheless do convincingly dramatize some of the basic issues and problems in the higher education of women, and they do provide insight and stimulation for taking next steps.

The what, how, and where of education for women aside, the theme running through the papers that stimulated me most concerned the mores of our society which sanction more higher education for more men than for women. This sanction is not based on the assumption that men are more capable of learning or need more formal education than women for fulfillment as persons, homemakers, or citizens. It operates on the premise that man is the principal breadwinner. This is decreasingly true.

We now have an economy in which one-third of the labor force is women, and the demand for womanpower at the professional, semi-professional, and technical levels is growing steadily. This change in our occupational outlook may bring as many women as men into higher education programs during the decade into which we are entering.

We graduate from high school each year 1.5 million students, and the number of girls exceeds the number of boys by nearly 100,000. And it is common knowledge that as a group, girls graduate with higher grades than boys. Nevertheless, the mores of our society sanction sending two boys through college for each girl so educated. It may well be that by the end of the decade this trend will be reversed by the increased demand for professionally trained women. It is inconceivable that we can afford to continue much longer a practice which denies full educational development to some of our most talented youth merely because they are women.

It would be ironical if materialism and vocationalism come to be the social forces that equalize the number of men and women attending our colleges and universities. Real educational statesmanship will be required to blend professional education for women with the occupational education they will continue to need as mothers and homemakers, and still leave enough time for education for personal fulfillment in the realms of civic, ethical, and spiritual development.

ERNEST V. HOLLIS
Director, College and University Administration Branch,
United States Office of Education

PREFACE

The role of the educated woman in the future is a provocative topic today and should become increasingly so within the next several years. The life-pattern of American women has been altered almost to a new way of life since their grandmothers' day, and to some extent, since the last generation. The change is all for the better, but it comes not without new challenges.

A renewed emphasis on the strategic place of educated women in our society is already with us. Recent research has reflected the place for enlightened and educated women in America, and mass media have been discussing the modern day woman in her modern day setting, but perhaps the most potent evidence comes from the young girls themselves. The fact is that more and more young women are *wanting* to become educated and more and more young women *are* being educated.

This book explores some of the basic challenges in trying *properly* to educate women for their increasingly significant role in society, and it presents the latest thinking by some of America's leading spokesmen in the area.

Such an array of outstanding talent, united to present their collective thinking on this lively subject, is the result of a commemorative program held in 1960 at the Mississippi State College for Women during its seventy-fifth anniversary. As the first publicly supported women's college in America, the Mississippi State College for Women wished to rededicate itself to its tradition of leadership and service. Through many commemorative programs, but especially through the formal symposium on "The Education of Women"—the source spring for this volume—the college wished to provide a permanent contribution to the higher education of women.

If one can believe commendations of the symposium, the event was significantly successful. Its ultimate success, however, can only be measured by the impact of the messages to a larger audience. For this reason this book is respectfully submitted.

The book follows closely the format of the symposium. Chapter titles have been changed, and chapters 10 and 11 were written by the editors. Since the original audience of the symposium was primarily college girls, the valid reasoning for the proper support of the higher education of women was not highlighted. But, as the proper investing in the higher education of women was a strategic aspect of the total anniversary celebration, Chapter 10 is designed to explore some of the problems of this very basic part of the educational enterprise. A challenge, then, for all to invest more in the education of women for all institutions, but especially for the women's colleges, so that the job may be accomplished with the success it deserves, is therefore a vital part of this chapter. Only when this goal is realized can the objectives of this book become a reality.

With the background, purpose and scope of this book already described, it remains, then, for the editors (1) to tell to whom this book is addressed, (2) to express their appreciation to all those who had a part in making this book possible, (3) to manifest gratitude for the privilege of editing the work, and (4) to explain how the thinking and views expressed are singularly attached to the authors.

First of all, this work should attract those who are interested in the higher education of women. The book is in no way exclusively aligned with the colleges for women—private or public—although many fine opinions as to their value are hinted at or stated with conviction throughout the book. For this reason, those educators interested in higher education in general might also find this volume valuable. Much of what has been written applies to the higher education of all—equally to men as well as to women.

This book might find itself very much at home in the hands of America's educated women—not only the contemporary leaders of society, but all who have the great potential to serve. Today's educated woman might especially be challenged with a true sense of purpose and dedication for realizing her own destiny, and at the same time—as an inherent part of her educational concept— for doing more for her family and home and for stepping out into the community and letting her influence be felt as far as her talents allow. As significantly, our present educated women might be challenged to assist in the furthering of more highly educated women for the future.

Since the addresses from which the manuscripts came were basically and essentially presented to a college girl audience, a young woman in college today might find this work especially enlightening. Because she is presently in the midst of this special world of college, she might be able to reflect and to consider if she is *actually* making the best use of her time, and if she is truly realizing all the objectives which she and the authors might agree are sound for the college girl. The book might be most valuable also for girls in college today to gain a perspective about their world of college and how they fit into it. It is especially meaningful to them as to the part they might play, as a group enjoying a college education, once they graduate from the halls of ivy.

While this volume is not a guidance book to college, the serious minded students in the secondary schools, their parents and especially high school guidance counselors, might find some very potent insight into colleges, what they are doing, what they are trying to do for the future, why a college education is important for women, and what they might do with their education.

The book also shows most favorably the role women's colleges play in educating women, their leadership and their potential. Because the type of schooling required to educate properly the women of today and tomorrow involves a reasonable investment for all institutions of higher learning, it would seem that this volume might serve convincingly as supplementary material to American business and industrial leaders, foundation executives, philanthropists, alumnae, and friends of education, who might be willing in the future to invest a more proportionate share in the education of women.

Secondly, we should like to express appreciation to all who have helped to make this work possible:

To Charles P. Hogarth, president of the Mississippi State College for Women, who initially gave approval of the idea for the original symposium.

To the members of the symposium committee, on which the senior editor had the privilege of chairmanship: Mrs. Alice James Gatchel, Miss Marguerite Goen, Dr. Frank Herndon, Dr. Irvin Weaver, Dr. Ellene Ransom, Dr. Mary Kate Miller, Dr. Willard Mishoff, Mrs. Nancy McHaney, Dr. Ottis Skipper, Mr. David Snipes, Miss Mary Wilson, and students Beth Brown, Martha Nelson, Kay Moseley, Betty Lynn Newcomb, Judy Stovall, Suenette Anderson, Sandra Marlin, Diane Rodgers, Frances Mobley, and Carolyn Stokes.

Most important of all, to the speakers themselves, for without their thinking and their efforts, the symposium could not have been the tremendous success that it was, and without their generous permission to have their papers published, this volume could not have become a reality.

To the office staff: Mr. Oscar Banks, Jr., Mr. Bill Bankston, Miss

Charlotte Miller, Mrs. Susan Merritt, Miss Martha Nelson, Mrs. Betty
Jo Stewart, and all student assistants who worked under severe
pressure to get this material done.   Especial appreciation goes to
Miss Cary Dowdle, for doing most of the typing of the Symposium
project and the manuscripts.

To Carroll B. Hanson, Director of Publications, U.S. Office of
Education, and Dorothy Roe, formerly Women's Editor of Associated
Press, who provided the symposium with outstanding question and
answer and summary sessions.

To college presidents Dr. Robert E. Lee, Dr. Freeman H. Beets,
Mr. Joseph E. Gibson, Dr. McFerran Crowe, and Dr. J. I. Riddle
for their generous assistance in recording the various sessions, and
to the many Deans of Women across the country, and to the American
Association of University Women.

Thirdly, the editors are grateful for the opportunity to share in
this volume. If the idea for the symposium and for this book originated
with them, the respective contributors with their provocative thinking
have done the lion's share in nourishing the concept into a reality.

Finally, since this is a collaborative work, the individual authors
are responsible for their own statements, and it was not inherent in
the purpose of this volume, or the symposium, that each author
agree. Even as editors, while we do most heartily concur with most
of the thinking, we do not agree with all that is stated in this volume.
Nor should every word herein be considered as necessarily the educational philosophy of the Mississippi State College for Women.

It is our sincere hope that everyone connected with the writing
and production of this project can feel a very true sense of involvement.

LEO C. MULLER
OUIDA GEAN MULLER

University of Buffalo
Buffalo, New York

CONTENTS

ABOUT THE CONTRIBUTORS

KATE HEVNER MUELLER, a noted psychologist, writer and lecturer, is professor of education at Indiana University. In 1956 she received the Delta Kappa Gamma $1,000 award for outstanding writing in education for her book, *Educating Women For a Changing World*. She has held positions at the University of Minnesota, the University of North Carolina, and the University of Chicago where she received her Ph.D.

FRANK A. ROSE became president of the University of Alabama after serving as president of Transylvania College. In 1955 he was voted one of the nation's ten outstanding men. He has lectured at Chatauqua, New York, and has taught philosophy at Transylvania. A member of the board of directors of American Universities Field Staff Program, he is also a curator of the Henry Clay Memorial Foundation. He holds an LL.D. from the University of Cincinnati and a Litt.D. from the University of Alabama.

SEYMOUR A. SMITH, the president of Stephens College, enjoys a rich background of education both here and abroad. A native New Yorker, he holds a Ph.D. from Yale and has served as a member of the Divinity faculty there. Under a Hazen grant, he did a study of British and European universities. His works include *The American College Chaplaincy, You in the University*, and *Religious Cooperation in the State Universities*. For four years he was the executive director of the National Council on Religion in Higher Education.

GRELLET C. SIMPSON is chancellor of Mary Washington College of the University of Virginia. The holder of a Ph.D. degree, he has served as dean of the faculty at Randolph-Macon College. Interrupting his career during World War II, he worked with the Red Cross in the United States and Italy.

EDNA P. AMIDON is director of the Home Economics Education Branch in the U.S. Office of Education. Co-author of *Learning To Care for Children*, she spent some time in Germany following World War II helping reorganize home economics education in that country. She has taught at the University of Missouri and the University of Minnesota where she received her M. S. She is a recipient of the service award of the American Vocational Association.

ANNA L. ROSE HAWKES, the president of the American Association of University Women, has marked her career in education by service with Mills College, George Washington University, the U. S. Advisory Commission on Educational Exchange, the Unesco General Conference in Paris, and the 1955 White House Conference on Education. She is the author of *Ability in Relation to School Progress* and co-author of *An Experiment in Responsible Learning* and *Through the Dean's Open Door*. She received her Ph.D. from Columbia.

ANNE ROE, a lecturer in the Graduate School of Education at Harvard University, is noted for her psychological research in the areas of intelligence, occupations, alcohol education, and foster children. A Guggenheim fellow, she has authored six books including *The Psychology of Occupations, The Making of a Scientist,* and *Science Begins at Home.* She received her Ph.D. from Columbia University.

MARGUERITE W. ZAPOLEON, a consultant in vocational guidance, was a special assistant in the Women's Bureau of the U. S. Department of Labor until she turned to full-time writing and lecturing. Before going into government service she was a vocational counselor with the Cincinnati school system. Her M.A. is from American University, and two previous degrees, one in engineering, are from the University of Cincinnati. She is the author of *The College Girl Looks Ahead.*

HAROLD TAYLOR became president of Sarah Lawrence College at the age of 30. In 1959 he resigned to write, think and study. After receiving his Ph.D. from the University of London when he was 23, he spent a year writing and traveling in Europe. Upon his return to the U.S. he taught philosophy at the University of Wisconsin and served with the Office of Scientific Research and Development during World War II. He is the author of several books.

LEO C. MULLER has in recent years been directing his interests toward the advancement of higher education. He is assistant to the Vice-Chancellor for Planning and Development and Director of University Relations at the University of Buffalo. He holds a bachelor's degree in philosophy from Loyola University, a master's in school administration and journalism from Louisiana State University, and is a candidate for the doctorate degree at Indiana University.

OUIDA GEAN MULLER holds a cum laude degree in journalism from Mississippi Southern College, where she was active in student affairs and edited the campus weekly. She earned her master's degree (with honors) in guidance from Indiana University. A former high school English teacher and associate Sunday editor of a daily newspaper (Jackson, Miss., *State Times*), she is a co-author, with her husband, of *College for Coeds* (Pitman Publishing Corp., New York, 1960). She has also contributed chapters to two forthcoming textbooks, *Introduction to Journalism* and *Principles of Advertising.*

WHAT IT'S ALL ABOUT

Kate Hevner Mueller

The fundamental question in 1885 about women's education is probably still the first question in 1960: Why should women be educated?

At the beginning of that century the answers were often shocked protests: "If women learn to write they might forge their husbands' signatures. If they learn to read they would neglect their housework." Women soon discovered that it was better not to ask questions, much better just to bustle around and get the college founded. By the middle of the century, protests even from the educators themselves were still loud and strong: it would be dangerous to admit women as coeds, both to the men students and to the women themselves; there would be riots and scandals and faintings and loss of revenue. By 1885, with the many private women's colleges in the North and East, with women trickling into some of the state universities, and with women actually allowed to vote in the pioneer state of Wyoming, a few states were beginning to realize that the persistent demands of women for learning could best be met by establishing their own state colleges for women.

What an amazing story of women these seven decades have to tell! And it is always the same story. Women have wanted to learn, to work, to vote, and there have always been some few who have worked against great odds to achieve these goals for themselves, and following them, other women who merely accepted and enjoyed them; and always there were millions of men and women who organized themselves to stop women from gaining these simple privileges.

The women pioneers of these seven decades were intelligent and experienced, and they tried to win over their opponents by reason, by gentle persuasion and by slow and painful organization. Their opposition has always had more power and more money. They have hated forward looking women, thrown cabbage and tomatoes at them, imprisoned them, denied them, exhorted them, and above all they have scorned and ridiculed them. They have called them hatchet-faced and laughed at their clothes. They have paid them lower salaries and denied them the good jobs.[2] Yet nothing their enemies have done has really been effective. The opposition continues, though it sometimes goes underground, the old jokes are revised, tempers and battles are lost and won, but the gains in privileges and rights and workers continue forward as slowly and relentlessly as time itself. Each generation sees more women working for longer periods, at better jobs, in new occupations. Time and sheer numbers seem to be always on the woman's side. Likewise time and the inevitable weight of the culture will guarantee them ultimate success, even though success, when it catches up with them, may have a new and very strange definition. In the meantime, most women seem to be quite happy with this present slow and comfortable rate of progress.

There have been many obvious changes in the circumstances of women's lives in seven decades. Two world wars, one great depression and several smaller recessions, and increasing technology have accelerated the changes. More women are working outside the home than ever before. They are pushed out of the home because housekeeping has been streamlined and lightened and because our children begin their social life outside the home at a very early age. Women are also pulled into work because of the attractive jobs at good wages, because their earnings are needed to attain a better standard of living, and because they are discontented with home life and find a much more interesting and useful life beside their husbands in the working world. Today the *median* family is a two income family. The non-working wives in our society are fast becoming a minority group.

I am, of course, fully aware that there are strong differences of opinion. I am not prepared to argue whether the typical college girl of today will work 20, or 25, or 30 years of her life, whether in the future the woman who does not work will be 1 in 8 or 1 in 9.[3] Moreover, I can observe that there are certain geographical regions, classes of society and age groups where women hold very steadfastly to their traditional ways of life. We know that women are more aggressive in the cities, in the North and Northeast and West, and in the higher socio-economic classes. Other women are more relaxed, which is the way men prefer them. But these statistical details are indications only of the *rate* of our progress. Its *fact* has never been denied by any of the social scientists who study it. Indeed, the trend has been not so much real opposition, as a nostalgic reluctance for admitting that it is there. And this very reluctance itself is one of the good things about it. We could not enjoy the triumphs of our progress, our rockets and antibiotics, our great cities and their career women were it not for the white church steeples, the sulphur-and-molasses, and the buxom little home bodies to tie us firmly to our long and glorious past. We all want progress of course, but not too fast, not with unseemly and disorganizing haste, and that is the way we will probably get it.

In this world of slow but undoubtedly accelerating change, what are the proper aims of higher education for women, and especially for a woman's college at the beginning of the 1960's? This question is very complex since many different kinds of colleges are needed. Higher education must preserve and transmit the culture of our own special brand of affluent American democratic society. It must teach our college women to enjoy and be happy living in it, to be healthy, wealthy, and wise in it, and to cherish it and pass it along undiminished to their children. Higher education must also be the conscience of our civilization and be responsible not only for keeping it intact, but for making it better, so that in the next 75 years, that is, in the year 2035, our grandchildren will be thankful that our education was right, was the best possible education for posterity, as well as for us.

However, let us first consider, not our grandchildren but only education today, college women moving from various classrooms, English and algebra, and history and art. These classes represent our culture, the best that our civilization has produced, the knowledge that is current among the best people. They include the books we have read, the science we have achieved, the music and art we love, and of course, the professional training we need to earn our living. Some of what we are taught gets a bit outdated and useless, some of it is inadequate and some of it even misleading, but most of it is not too ill chosen, and good or bad, difficult or easy, we are committed to it, for this is *our* culture, our society, our nation, our very decade.

Investigations are continuously in process to measure the actual gains made by students on the college campus. Researchers working in the colleges have issued the following conclusion: Whenever the students are happy in their work, satisfied with their homes and nicely free from worry and frustration, they are not learning, and in fact, in many cases it is not even possible to educate them.

Without puzzlement, discontent, and anxiety there is no progress in learning.

They hold that seniors in contrast to freshmen are not quite so chubby and bouncy and brash, a little more poised and skeptical and tolerant, less modest, more assertive and a little more flexible. But they doubt that college has taught them these virtues. Young women would have learned them anyway in the years from 17 to 21, no matter where they were, from four years more of life experience, four years of gracious living, at home, with some travel, some reading and shopping and do-it-yourself-work, or perhaps volunteer service.

David Riesman fears,[4] and Nevitt Sanford confirms[5] that even though the senior is more liberal, more individualized by reason of her passage through college, the change will disappear when she leaves the campus and returns to the regulated larger society. A few years back in the old home town or with a new young family in a different town and the alumnae have slipped back into their old complacent ways of thinking. It is too much to hope that individuality and independence, tolerance and intellectual openmindedness could hold out against the overwhelming weight of the current heritage, against all the tradition and folklore of our twentieth century materialistic, competitive, romantic culture which fiction, advertising, sports, television, bridge table, supermarket, and office gossip continually press upon college bred youth.

How difficult it is to accept the theory that the actual process of learning is not pleasant. To be sure, many bright young women have found the process of getting good grades a very simple, pleasant, and easy one. But this is not the true process of learning. It is merely socialization, absorbing the culture. The pace is slow; there are such excellent audio-visual aids that learning the plot of *War and Peace,* the dates of the Crusades, the table of chemical elements, even acquiring a good French accent is about as easy as "learning" to buy a certain breakfast cereal, or to wash one's hair with some special soap. It is even possible that many of these accomplishments could be acquired during sleep, given a good loudspeaker in each dormitory. Certainly many good habits and manners are acquired in this way, in a kind of cultural osmosis. In contrast, much of college learning is actually unlearning. College English courses, for example, are needed to correct the errors in speech and writing accumulated in 17 years of absorbing that less-than-standard English which our home town cultures have imposed on us. History, literature, and economics must often revolutionize the earlier notions gained from our more provincial life experiences. The transformation from a local citizen to a national or international citizen will prove difficult and disturbing. There is no learning without tension, frustration, effort, strain, and doubt. To be a serious intellectual in today's college is to be exceptional. The good student is one who is willing to work and willing to be different. She must feel her superiority and admit it, when she is alone, when she is with her classmates, and especially when she is with men.

There is an indication that at least the college years have taught the student how to be healthy, how to be flexible and adaptable, how to make the best of the world as she finds it, how to get along pleasantly with other people, how to achieve material success, stability and peace of mind. In college she acquires some facts, enlarges her vocabulary, widens her acquaintance, and learns some skills, especially vocational skills. Data show that the college graduates earn much more, vote more often with the winning majorities, live longer, and have fewer divorces.[6] This we can assume means good mental health for themselves and their families, and continued economic prosperity for the nation. Insofar as these things are acceptable and admirable for a stable society, their education has been good.

The students and the alumni would perhaps settle for these advantages, but many educators would not. In their college catalogues they have described far different goals, and in spite of the fact that few of these goals are usually accomplished, college presidents persist in writing about them, hoping perhaps for a miracle. And the students keep right on profiting from the prestige of going to their chosen colleges, passing, and sometimes even enjoying their courses, and marrying each other and sending their children to dear old Alma Mater. But the student's values, his purposes, his imperatives, even his reading habits, are little changed, if at all.

Educators also hoped for but apparently did not give their students a real dedication to the intellectual life. This does not mean that women should become blue stockings or bookworms or greasy grinds or whatever the current slang might dub them, nor even that they enter a learned profession or devote their lives to research or teaching. It means that they live by the mind, that they exercise reason and judgment, that they investigate, meditate, and discuss the events of their time before they take any action. It means that they enjoy leisure time activities which are intellectual in character, the fine arts rather than the escape activities.

Such pursuits and interests are those of the mature rather than the juvenile, the independent and thoughtful, not the dependent and conforming personality. They are also precisely what the college youth himself means when he says that he wants to be a real personality, an individual. Human maturity surely consists of developing to full capacity that one aspect of man which distinguishes him from animals, his brain.

For man, in contrast to animals, can speak and read and write. He can preserve his past, learn from it, build his own society and improve on it. Man is the only animal with a conscience, the only one that can realize the meaning of life, the only animal that knows he is going to die, that distinguishes the present from the future. Animals can be taught a kind of right and wrong, at least how to achieve rewards and avoid punishment, but not to appreciate the beautiful, the true, the good. These are human qualities, and full humanity means cultivating them, building a life and a home and a community around them, and by means of them. It means learning, thinking and creating for the sheer pleasure of developing and enjoying a fuller intellectual life.

But to be an individual, an intellectual individual, in our present day culture is possibly one of the most difficult feats ever required of man. All the weight of the culture is against it. Society can ask a man to die for his country or his beliefs, and thousands have done so, for the culture sanctions it, even approves it. But to live, constantly opposing oneself to the mass of daily habit and custom, to endure the difficulties, defy the disapproval, suffer the inconveniences—this is asking more of the individual than most of us unheroic human beings would be able to give.

It might be imagined otherwise. It is conceivable that colleges, receiving the best of our youth, might in four years instill in them not only facts and skills and sophistication, but the habits and attitudes of mind which would convert them into the thinking, intellectually dominated animals they were surely meant to be. This would mean three great changes in higher education: (1) A selection of students on the basis of different intellectual and personality traits than are now used for their selection in 1960, (2) a different intellectual climate and more inducement to intellectual endeavor than we find on most of our campuses, and (3) different curricula with new subject matter and more imaginative methods of communicating them. Let us look more closely at these three conditions.

(1) Today colleges select their students on the basis of intelligence and school achievement from the applicants who are attracted to them, that is, from the middle and upper middle classes. Even the new and nationwide scholarship programs can do little more than this, although the broader scope of their efforts and financing plus the cooperation they have engendered have no doubt improved on the results that the colleges could have achieved alone. We are far indeed from placing in our colleges just those seventeen and eighteen-year-olds who can achieve the intellectual qualities of the mature human adult, who long to work hard, who are willing to be exceptional and resist the easy blandishments of their society. As yet in 1960, we can scarcely describe these qualities, much less measure them.

(2) Few colleges today create the intellectual climate which could transform these students in the manner that the educator has hoped. Robert Hutchins described the college campus at its worst: "Our purpose is to turn out well tubbed young Americans who know how to behave in an American environment. Association with one another and with gentlemanly professors in beautiful buildings will, along with regular exercise, make our students the kind of citizens our country needs. These are exactly what is advertised by every resort hotel." Nevitt Sanford gives one of the reasons why it could hardly be otherwise: The student at entrance has lived in his culture for seventeen or eighteen years, and brings it with him to the campus along with his hats and shoes, his camera and record collection. He carries with him his determination to secure the best things in life for himself and his family, his well nourished appetite for thrills, his desire for intimacy, his mixture of rebellion and admiration for his elders, his complacency with his peers.

And the institutions of his society also pursue him to the campus. The fraternity and club life divert him. In a mobile community he is regularly drawn away every other weekend to his home or to other adventures. He learns how to shortcut academic difficulties, how to learn easily, rather than well, and how to keep the faculty in their proper place. Sanford tells us: "It is the increasing penetration into the colleges of the prevalent in our culture outlook that creates the great educational problem of today. It is not just the increasing numbers; it is the very real prospect—given continued prosperity—that higher and higher proportions of entering students will lack any special motivation for scholarship, will tend to perpetuate in the college society precisely those unintellectual virtues which it is the job of the college to combat."[8]

(3) The curricula themselves are often anti-intellectual. Sometimes they are watered down, or sugared off, or jazzed up to suit the interests of the faculty or the current tastes and demands. Sometimes they are an unwieldy accumulation of compromises, and sometimes cheaply mass-produced. They may be ponderous, or esoteric, or they may be ill chosen or disorganized. Some of them are quite good, and many of them are not at all bad, just badly taught.

Many plans exist for reorganizing the current college curricula; we can give our attention only to those areas of most interest to women. A liberal education today, as always, seems the most appropriate for women, but it must be a liberal education which escapes the stuffy tradition and puts the old subject matter in new lights, for new uses. Women, especially young women, even more than young men, need to know thoroughly their own society because of the unequal pressures that society places upon women in competition for satisfactions and success. They need to understand its forces, what is behind them, what it takes to change them, and what are its predictable trends. Women must learn history not merely to appreciate the past but to interpret the present and foresee the future.

Women need to know how long they can expect to work, what job opportunities are best, what kinds of satisfactions and salaries these jobs will bring, what disappointments, hazards, and strains they will offer. As they feel the pressures to marry, in fact to marry early and have children, they must know what will be expected of mothers of the future *in addition to* care of children, where the expectations and attitudes come from, what treatment to expect from fathers, husbands, sons, employers, each different than the other, from advertisers or manufacturers who want to sell them goods, from the older generations of mothers and aunts who may or may not be realistic. All youths, men or women, have strong needs for companionship, security, intimacy; but these must not be sacrificed to other later needs of adults for recognition, or self expression or independence.

Women have not capitalized in their curricula on the value of professional training as a liberating force in their education. Men's education is frankly *for* something, for earning a living. For them the so-called liberal education has never been central but always **for** supporting, or enhancing or preparing for their vocational purposes. In a society such as ours, in the future as we envisage it, to hold that any kind of education for women is good *in itself* is a supercilious, dilettante point of view, misleading to student and to society. The woman of the future will work, and only an education which fits her for this life work can free her from the crippling pressures of her surrounding culture. She needs the liberal education exactly as a man needs it, to prepare her for the varied aspects of her future life. To claim otherwise is to push her into a false position and leave her defenseless against some of her most significant hazards.[9]

But higher education must not only transmit, it must also improve and enhance the culture, give more and more of its members a satisfying life, not only raising their standards of living but also raising the human values that they hold. To do this higher education must train society's leaders and generate a climate of opinion in the whole society which will give its leaders an opportunity to accomplish their ends.

Leadership has been a much abused and misunderstood concept, but it is obvious that the college population as a whole comprises the leaders of our current American society. They are not exactly a meritocracy, as Russia tries to arrange, because the college educated have not been selected for their education according to their merit. They have volunteered for education, and for its privileges, not its responsibilities. Leadership, however, is expected from all of us although most of us are actually followers. Yet as followers, paradoxically, we are performing one of the most important leadership activities. It is our special job as followers to generate that necessary appreciation and tolerance and enthusiasm which alone make it possible for more aggressive and imaginative leaders to accomplish their results.

The leaders needed by our society, the leaders we expect our colleges to train, are divided into many categories and many levels. All professional persons are automatically leaders: the good teachers, lawyers, pianists, architects, physicians, nurses, who are successful in their chosen occupations, bringing honor to it, adding to its knowledge, improving its services. This is a very necessary and honorable kind of leadership. Such professional women leaders are all the more important because they can also create a happy family life within the home and demonstrate to their male colleagues that women can be happy and useful in both roles, just as the best men of our generation demonstrate that they can be successful in their occupations and as fathers and homemakers within the family circle.

Another kind of leadership charged by tradition to women in our society is that of maintaining both social skills and social conscience. For this, they need not only the conviction, the determination to make the world a good place to live, which most of them have, but the knowledge, especially a hard-core sophisticated knowledge, of what societal forces stand in our way of accomplishing these ends. Women have not been good learners in this field. Many hard working, well meaning women have marched and rung door bells and signed petitions, only to find that dishonest elections defeated their good cause. The volunteer worker may find herself occupied with mere leg-work and busy-work and trivialities while others decide policies (often bad ones) and make decisions, wise or otherwise, in a society where social planning and professional services have outdated much of her efforts.

But of even greater importance to women students of our generations is the leadership in developing a personal and creative fulfillment, an appreciation for the truly feminine, introspective, aesthetic, affective aspects of life. Leisure time, we are told, is the most important product of our technology, and in our society there is little evidence that it is being used for true personal happiness, for real societal gain. We are too prone to entertainment rather than creativity. We keep our arts alive on social prestige, rather than understanding, on refinement of technique rather than expressiveness. We cultivate our how-to-do-it hand crafts to the exclusion of the more intellectual fine arts.

Our teaching in both religion and aesthetics has not been appropriate to the intellectual level of our students. We have taught them indirectly, by story and history, by the accoutrements, not the essentials of these experiences. The spiritual qualities and the aesthetic life are closely related in the personality, and their concepts and skills require the same kind of rigorous intellectual endeavor. The psychology of their learning is the same as for any other kind of academic achievement. We have leaned on inspiration and emotion where we should have emphasized content and form. When these are mastered, the possibilities for continued enjoyment are infinite, the appetite for growth is insatiable. This is the sphere where women's leadership is most needed, most rewarding.

Of course, our women's world needs *also* leaders who are statesmen in the best sense of that word, statesmen both in their public or professional work and in their private citizenship activities, women with so much zeal for service to mankind, so much vitality and social skill that their leadership extends beyond their own home communities to the larger state and national and even international world of action and ideas. They will write, speak, study, do research, and publish, serve as educational leaders, or they may work in politics, achieve high elective positions, serve as judges, senators, labor leaders. Some will go into the business world as managers and entrepreneurs. Many, and there should be more, will continue to serve in the arts where some of our best leaders are women— poets, novelists, painters, and sculptors, pianists and singers, actors and producers. Science also owes much to such learned and dedicated women.

We hardly know, as we also do not know about men, what personal and intellectual qualities, what motivations, experiences and education, have produced these special geniuses, these admirable and necessary leaders. We do know that it takes high ability, some plain good luck, and a lot of energy. Many persons simply do not have the metabolism for high production. We do know at least two qualities that are required. The first is hard work, long hours of it after others have gone to the movies, or to their gardening or television or bridge parties, or have just simply gone to bed. The second is the willingness to turn her back quite ruthlessly on past successes, on all the ties that bind her to her present satisfactions and her accumulated past and to embark on new adventures. Warner and Abegglen[10] called this a kind of departure from everything safe and steady. It is the highest possible sense of adventure, the willingness to take every chance. Others have said that it is the ultimate freedom, the truly liberal, the ability to rise above the culture to judge it and criticize it. Still others, as Mary McCarthy in *The Florentines*, recognized in it that insatiable human desire to excel, to compete, but not to compete with others, rather a higher endeavor to exceed even one's own self.

Whatever it is, we respect and acclaim it, and we serve and follow it gladly. We want and need more of it. Is it too much to hope that each college could produce in each year just one such graduating senior? She may not be that well dressed, well rounded person that our society so much admires. She may wear funny hats or be unpleasantly mousey and queer. Or she may be so beautiful and dominating that we all hate her methods and envy her success. But she may achieve something for the future day by diligence or ruthlessness or good luck, or pure genius, and we shall rejoice with her and honor her accordingly. There must be one or two, maybe three or four on every college campus. All we can safely say is that we can't recognize them *now*.

In our thinking about 75 years of history and looking 75 years into the future, we should note one significant modern comment about ourselves: "We are perhaps too near the revolution of the women— probably the greatest social revolution in the true sense, that the world has even seen—to understand all its ramifications." Joyce Cary made this statement as long ago as 1951, and it is not so much his announcing and labelling of that movement that is significant, but rather his acceptance of the fact that we do not recognize nor understand what is happening to our world, our American world of men and women.

It is foreign to our present day habits of thought to see ourselves as living in the midst of a revolution. It is commonplace to say that we are on the brink of great discoveries. We speak confidently about our "breakthroughs" past and future, not one, but many: in medicine, the Salk vaccine and others; in manufacturing, the automatic factory; in air service, the jets and the rockets, the astronauts, etc.

We are all too familiar with the economists' prophesies about women, but they can forecast only the numbers and the salaries, nothing about the effect of these jobs on the personalities of the working women, on the attitudes of their husbands toward them, and the behavior of the children, which is their revolutionary aspect. These aspects are more problematical and speculative, but they are also the things that we are expected to worry about, if we are to give good service to our women and our country today.

A revolution is something quite different from mere progress in scientific ventures. Progress goes straight forward, but revolution is the effect of that progress as it turns back on the human beings who experience it to produce new thinking in them. We enjoy our progress most fully when it is relatively superficial, when it rests lightly and comfortably on the more permanent elements of our lives. It is when our thinking and feeling are changed, when convictions and attitudes are shaken, that we speak of revolution.

During the centuries of history the mutations in the thinking of man about himself, his government, his welfare, and his relations with other people have never been logical and linear and straight-forward. They have zig-zagged their way forward, dodging inter-ference and seizing opportunities like a good football player carrying the ball. Man has finally overcome, for example, the old ideas of inherited power, of the divine right of kings. It was a long and complex revolution in action, thought and feeling. More recently as history goes, man has been struggling with an industrial revolution, the displacement of the flexible individual worker by the inflexible but mechanically efficient machine. Man has not yet solved the problems of this industrial upheaval and is still arguing about the right to work, about labor in politics, about monopolies and feather-bedding, tariffs and inflationary practices. Industry accepts the practices and improve-ments which this kind of technology brings with it long before the public is ready to absorb or compromise or accept the thinking, the theory, the attitudes that go with it. The changes in methods and practice seem always to precede the changes in theory, which are inevitable but develop more slowly, as a cultural lag.

We are likewise in our diplomacy forced to deal practically with the rising importance of underdeveloped countries. Their claims and problems are effective in international politics although we have not yet been able to settle on an acceptable foreign policy for dealing with them. Disruptive as they are, we are forced to accept them and to readjust our ideologies to these new national movements—a true revolution in our social thought.

Events of the present in regard to women are also forcing a revolu-tion in our attitudes and thinking. Two streams of events and cir-cumstances are pushing it: the economic facts of women working and a series of breakthroughs in our scientific knowledge about the human mind and personality.

James M. Barrie in *The Twelve Pound Look* and *What Every Woman Knows* gave our grandmothers an inkling of the effect on the feminine personality when she has an independent income. James Thurber and a long line of following cartoonists find delight in the *War Between The Sexes*. But these humorous repercussions from the economic effects of women voting and working have been more seriously studied by modern social science; and the attitudes of men and women toward each other have been much altered by the know-ledge that there are no sex differences in intelligence, ability, creative-ness, and other talents, that whatever differences do appear can be traced to differences in the culture, in the pressures of society to which the two sexes are very differently subjected.

From small beginnings, social scientists have now turned to more extensive investigations of the human personality. Such studies are now the preoccupation of psychologists, and even business and recreation and education are busy on personality and human relations research. They work also on the feeling and emotions and personality development, and their analyses of love, mother love, and romantic love, not yet widely known, are introducing grave uncertainties into traditional theories of child rearing.

Who can doubt that we are on the verge of a breakthrough also on the philosophy and methods of birth control? The so-called population "explosion" is actually an explosion in the realm of our thinking about these problems. Even in this country, in the most favored and affluent nation, we may be forced to revise our ideas about the size of our families.

One cannot prophesy, only speculate on the implications of these changes, the revolution in our theories about women, their independence, their status and roles; but sooner or later they must catch up with and overcome the feelings of dependency which have been the identifying mark of femininity for many a century. To achieve the same freedom as men from the pressures of the culture (which is after all, far from real freedom for either of the sexes) and to gain the same opportunities for self fulfillment, these are the ultimate fruits of the revolution in which we are all involved.

Togetherness, that conspiracy of publishers, advertisers, and manufacturers, has had its day; but there will be other conspiracies and women will fall for them because they, with their husbands, are spending their mental lives in the cute little prefabricated house which society holds out to them, not the real house of the intellect which they might have chosen. They will be happy in it, which we can in no way regret until the revolution creeps up on them. When it does, there will be new patterns of living, and college students will somehow learn them. We cannot predict what they may be, but one of them is so attractive that it might be worth consideration.

Today we have come to realize that life itself has its patterns and cycles. The period we call youth, the rising crescendo of our struggle to achieve the goals we have set for ourselves, actually thrusts itself well beyond the ages of twenty and thirty, and on into the forties. This is the extrovert, the masculine phase of our lives—when our major concerns are with external reality, education, vocational success, setting up our homes, having and rearing our children.

In the latter half of life, after 35 or 40, we are more poetic. We have time to contemplate; we have more money, more leisure, and we are more relaxed. Actually too, we have more grace and beauty and style. We wear our personalities, as our clothes, with more authority. Our voices are richer, our glance more direct, our features have more character, for our success and our individuality are stamped in our faces, in our general bearing. Our personalities at their best have not only variety but emotional depth, and we can give to the world whatever aspect or feeling we choose, withholding also whatever we choose, which youth cannot do. We know the sensuous flavor of tastes, sights, sounds, and movements, the emotional overtones of ideas, situations, and people, things which youth is too tense, too hurried, too uncertain to enjoy.

In youth we develop our doing and acquiring at the expense of feeling, reflecting, and enjoying. Psychiatrists might say that we develop our conscious at the expense of our unconscious. Only by adding the introvert, the thoughtful, the feminine, the aesthetic phase of human development (the real maturities of life), can we strike the balance which makes possible the individual man at his best, which guarantees full mental health and independence. The pressures of our society scarcely allow any of us, women or men, to achieve this until the second half of our lives. For most of us our competitive, aggressive "youth" is delayed far too long.

In our society during the present epoch, the greatest, the most unfortunate sex difference is not the physical, biological, or personality difference, real or imagined, but the differential pressures of our culture, which prevent *men* from developing the feminine and feeling side of their personalities and at the same time exclude *women* from achieving the masculine, extrovert, vocational successes which constitute our highest current values.

These pressures keep the man occupied with material achievement so fully and under such stress that his physical health is jeopardized, and the struggle is so prolonged that he can never retrieve his lost and undeveloped aesthetic capacities. Pressures, likewise, keep the woman from realizing her adventurous and earning potentials, and thus her full intellectual capacity. Both young men and young women wrestle valiantly but ineffectually with the problems of satisfying their honest desires for all human varieties of pleasure in the manner both personally satisfying and socially acceptable. They struggle only to reduce their tensions. Their striving for wholeness, personal stability, true individuality, for the meaning of life comes only much later when each personality, the masculine and the feminine, has become too inflexible, too one-sided to fulfill its human destiny.

Through many centuries and the most diverse cultures, human nature has never ceased to struggle for the ultimate meaning of life. Some find this meaning, this self fulfillment, in religion. Primitive peoples, living closer to nature, found their own simple and satisfying answers. The more intellectual our culture becomes, the more difficult the solution, the fewer those who achieve it, the later in our lives does this best-of-life come.

To achieve the better balance for man-at-his-best we must ask a vital question: what satisfaction in life do two marriage partners find exclusively in each other? How much is achieved through the partner, and how much through other persons, friends, relatives, business or club associates, or through intellectual or community achievements or business or household routines? How much in the affective life, aesthetic, religious, emotional, in dreaming or meditating? Does one or the other partner have larger, wider, richer experiences than the other? Does one live at a higher level of emotional or affective life, in a more intellectual environment, with stimulating problems and social contacts? Does one work harder or longer, dress better, have more frustration and worry, have more scope for action, more control over environment, more liking or disliking of life?

Each good marriage partner complements and shares with the other, but earns his independence in his own way. It is the exaggerated, inescapable dependence that is fatal to happiness and the good life. No one person can live his life only in terms of another. Our culture *today* gives no function to the dependent wife. Home life is no longer built from the inside out. The mother must go out into the culture to bring something back to make the home. To say otherwise is to say that we should be satisfied with conquering our own atmosphere and therefore keep out of the world of moons and planets.

Sooner or later, at 30 or 40 or 50, our world will decree that the wife will need a job. The smart young couple pushes the wife toward the same kind of professionally satisfying and well paid future as her husband, and at the same time (and what is much harder) pushes the husband into exploring his neglected affective and creative potentials.

Only the college which offers professional training along with its liberal and cultural courses can prepare today's young woman for her twentieth and twenty-first century life. Only a similar combination can properly educate the husband she is destined to have.

EDUCATION FOR WHAT?

Frank A. Rose

Let something go wrong in our world and immediately some Americans will suggest that education is the cure. From our national income, we will spend billions of dollars annually on education. But do we stop to ask ourselves this serious question, "Education for what?"

We have lately heard a great deal about Russian education and some fairly serious indictments of American education. "It is impossible to discover a man who believes that the right things were done to his mind," Mark Van Doren has said.[1]

"During the past forty or fifty years," declares Walter Lippmann, "those who were responsible for education have progressively removed from the curriculum of studies the western culture which produced the modern democratic state; that the schools and colleges have, therefore, been sending out into the world men who no longer understand the creative principle of the society in which they must live; that deprived of their cultural tradition, the newly western man no longer possesses on the form and substance of his own mind and spirit, the ideas, the premises, the rationale, the logic, the method, the values, or the deposited wisdom which are the genius of the development of Western civilization; that the prevailing education is destined, if it continues, to destroy Western civilization, and is in fact destroying it."[2]

These words constitute a pretty damaging indictment. While we would not all agree fully with them, we must agree that there is enough truth in them that we are sobered by their implications. The report on the survey conducted under the auspices of the Edward W. Hazen Foundation and published in Philip E. Jacob's book, *Changing Values in College,* reveals that there has been a definite decline in the moral and spiritual values of our modern college students and that an education in our colleges and universities is no guarantee of any improvement of personal values, but in the lives of some students there has been a rather substantial loss.

Perhaps we have not taken seriously enough our responsibility of educating the whole individual. A report of the Commission on Reform of German Higher Education speaks of the "necessity of making truly cultured, social, and civic-minded persons out of young academicians, and of bringing them to a consciousness of the ultimately religious foundations of life in our society, because without this deep ethical sense of obligation all human work and the progress of learning is in peril of self-annihilation."

The events of recent years have taught us convincingly that we are not going to live the next half century as comfortably and complacently as we have lived the last half. We are living in a world where our social, political, and economic values have been challenged by a ruthless opponent of great material strength. This position can be maintained only insofar as we are able to increase our intellectual and moral values to the place that they will enable us to face the great issues that will come before us.

The scientific and technological advances of more recent years make it imperative that our colleges and universities re-evaluate their educational philosophies and practices, study their participation in those practices, and seek to meet the responsibilities of these days. It seems to me that no college or university can claim exemption from these searching inquiries.

Many modern educators have been seriously disturbed by our inability to give to the leadership of the world the kind of human product that is capable of seeing the "whole" that is involved. Some of the questions being asked by the more serious educators are: Can we learn to welcome discipline when it is so easy to avoid it? Can we become sympathetic and understanding of the needs around the world, when it is more practical to be provincial? Can we become sons of God as well as sons of Man, when so much of success is recognized by the size of a man's house, the length of his automobile, and the amount of his account in the bank? These are some of the real questions facing modern education, and our answers to them may very well determine the quality of life in the last half of this century.

The quest for a basic educational philosophy or integrating principle has led to several attempts to what Frank Aydelotte has entitled, *Breaking the Academic Lockstep*. The Harvard Report on *General Education in a Free Society* sees in our cultural heritage the unifying core of a sound educational program. This report attempts to reconcile the three chief constituents of our cultural heritage, which are the ideal of the free man inherited from the ancient Greek civilization, which emphasizes the life of reason; the ideal of the Good Life contributed by the Hebraic-Christian faith, and the contributions to empirical knowledge through the scientific method of experimentation. Many colleges and some professional schools have strengthened their academic programs by developing large-unit, general education courses that would transmit the cultural heritage of Western civilization through a content-centered program of instruction.

An earlier school of thought was that found in the philosophy of John Dewey and practiced in most of our high schools and colleges. This view insists that student needs must be the basis of our modern curriculum. This approach requires an examination of the student's individual needs in preparing himself to enter a society in which he must earn a living, rear a family, meet the responsibilities of citizenship, and face the whole gamut of problems in modern civilization.

Another basic purpose of higher education is educating the Christian citizen. Most of our church colleges follow this concept. Its advocates hold that this philosophy includes all of the essentials of a sound educational program adequate for our society in this age of science, that it is broad enough to encompass all the elements of our cultural heritage, and that it provides the fullest approach to the individual needs of the student.

With these three fundamental philosophies in mind, many colleges are seeking to make the student a well-rounded, sensitive man, to make him a religious citizen, and to relate him effectively to all other men in the common life process. Then he becomes a specialist in the field of his professional interests.

Many educators are coming to realize the necessity of the student finding, in the academic community, devoted and interested people who are ready to listen and counsel him when he needs help. Systems of guidance are being initiated to enable the student to utilize the maximum of the educational resources during his four years. There is no substitute in the education process for the well-trained, devoted teacher who comes before the student challenged to remove the barriers of ignorance and prejudice and start him on the road to knowledge and self-realization.

Moral values are lacking in so many of our students because of the poor way in which they are taught. Part of this lack stems from the inability of some professors to teach, but much of it is due to the absence of a genuine commitment to the responsibilities of good teaching. Piety can never be a substitute for academic excellence, but there are some value judgments that can be made if the teacher sees his subject being taught as it is related to the whole of human life on our planet. Alfred North Whitehead informs us that "the real justification for a university is that it preserves the connection between knowledge and the zest for life, in that it unites the young and the old in the imaginative consideration of learning."[3]

Such changes in educational programs and emphasis indicate that educators are trying to shape their institutions in accordance with the most constructive change. They reveal the effort colleges are making to keep their educational philosophy alive and vital. It must be this way or we will not be able to provide the leadership that will be needed in an increasingly competitive society.

The urgency of our time is found in the acceleration with which crises come. We are all—teachers and students—going to give more than our normal efforts, or we will not have again an opportunity to aid so vitally the task that is before us. The success of our educational institutions is made necessary by our modern advances.

Before World War II, 200 miles per hour was speed, but today any of us can fly with 100 other passengers at 650 miles per hour. Recently I saw the plans for a commercial airliner that would fly 2500 miles per hour and I was shown the replica of a missile that would attain the speed of 18,000 miles per hour. This is the progress of pure scientific research and good engineering. Name any scientific field you wish, and on the drawing board there is a new discovery that makes the facilities of the present obsolete.

Whether we like it or not, we are what someone has called "a new Adam;" and life is not going to be easy in the modern "Garden of Eden." We are going to have to put new wine in the old wineskins.

Our universities must become centers of learning if they are going to have any relevance to our age. We have taken all too lightly our responsibility of turning out academicians who possess the abilities and knowledge to help us forge ahead in these many areas in which we are now lagging. We cannot keep shooting at the moon and missing it and retain confidence in our scientific and educational programs.

Nineteen million mentally ill people in the United States reveal that many tried to hit the moon of their careers and failed this, too. Juvenile delinquency, the high divorce rate, political bungling—these reveal an intellectual and moral weakness that informs us we have not been as successful as we would like to think.

We must adjust our programs of education and put new values into our old degrees. In speaking of the necessity of reshaping education, Dean Jerome Wiesner of the Massachusetts Institute of Technology, recently said that our schools must recognize one great need: "The social and economic upheavals now brought about by scientists and engineers make it imperative to educate our young men with an awareness of the social and economic consequences of their actions."

The principal task, then, is to develop in our most promising students the capacity to lead future technologies, the very nature of which are essentially unknown during the formal period of education. Just as scientific and technological institutions were created a century or more ago in response to the Industrial Revolution, so must we re-think the role and shape our institutions in response to the current revolution. To do less is to surrender our leadership to a ruthless foe in the race in which there will be no prizes for second place. General De Gaulle was right when he said: "I am not so concerned as to who will control the moon, as to how long it will take man to control himself."

3

WOMEN ARE PEOPLE

Seymour A. Smith

The Bible suggests that woman was created from the rib of a man.
From that day to this, at least in emergent western society, woman
has been seeking emancipation from a predominantly man's world.
Men may be inclined to quibble and insist that this is less and less a
man's world, and there is truth in this. Women have certainly made
considerable progress in establishing their own identity and independence in the past 100 years.

At superficial levels the emancipation of women has meant the
freedom to join in the conversation of men, to discard the veil, or to
cut their hair. More modern manifestations find women achieving
the dubious privilege of wearing trousers, which serve with varying
degrees of success the basic function of anatomical coverage; or in
smoking, drinking, or swearing so as to take umbrage of no man.

At more fundamental levels women have also made progress. It
has been only within this century that women secured the right to
vote, and with it, the right to take vigorous leadership in shaping
national policy, whether through the torchlight parades of a Carrie
Nation or the less spectacular but more sound efforts of a League of
Women Voters.

That women might be intelligent and tough enough to endure the
rigors of higher education has been a concession men have been
willing to make only within the past 100 years. The crusade to
open vocational and professional areas, other than schoolteaching or
typing, to women has begun to bear fruit only within my lifetime.
But it is now commonly accepted that women control the major resources of spending in our day and own more than 50 per cent of
the nation's wealth.

So there is some validity in the claims of the quibblers that this
is less and less a man's world.

While women may wave their hatchets as they lift a cry of triumph
and men may decry the sad state of affairs to which we have descended,
there is in this crusade of emancipation the disturbing possibility that

this is nothing more than the freedom *to be like a man*. By and large the education of women in America is based upon this premise. Certainly this has been true historically. Women's colleges patterned programs after those serving men. In all types of institutions young women and their adult guides were eager to demonstrate that women were competent to handle the same subject matter as men. They managed to do this effectively—perhaps too effectively. The traditionalists were prepared to let the matter rest there. But as traditional curricula were compromised in the interest of making all of higher education more "practical," programs were introduced which moved toward career outlets specifically designed for women: teaching, home economics, fashion design, business education, etc. But relatively few institutions moved beyond the "women's career" concept to challenge the male-dominated curriculum.

Occasionally an institution dared to suggest that a traditional discipline might be approached from a "woman's point of view," that it might be appropriate to enter the intricacies of economic principles from the perspective of the consumer rather than that of a banker or industrialist, or that marriage and the family might conceivably be approached as something a woman (or a man) might possibly encounter as a personal experience rather than as a dispassionate analysis of marriage customs of the Zulus or cold statistics of the interrelationship of socio-economic status to juvenile delinquency.

Even those institutions which had dared to venture forth, however timidly, along these lines have been brought up short by a current resurgence of concern for returning to "fundamentals" and a rush to recapture the assumptions of a tired Robert Hutchins that "education should be everywhere and always the same."

The pressures to bring order, simplicity and uniformity into higher education are immense. This is understandable in the midst of the chaos, complexity, and specialism which is characteristic of so much of higher education.

But so far as women are concerned, this is the time to strike a new blow for freedom, to suggest that a vigorous fresh challenge should be flung out to provide a real emancipation for women in our colleges and universities—thus to release the strangle hold of men which throttles a woman's fundamental integrity as a person when it is applied as a formula by which she is to prepare for the complicated, often paradoxical, and essentially different life which is hers.

We ought to question three fundamental assumptions which now underlie much of higher education for women.

To begin with, if we are to respect women for the different persons they are, we ought now to have another serious look at the time lock-step which currently fetters thinking about undergraduate education. Like superstitious folk of another day who developed elaborate rationalizations for magical numbers, modern educators have been hypnotized by the number *four* as being just the right number of years to encompass undergraduate programs beyond high school.

There are good historical reasons for this, and there is justification for developing some minimum standards, even if they are measured by only the number of hours per week in a four-year period a student can manage to sit through lectures of varying degrees of interest and usefulness.

The two-year colleges which appeared on the scene during this century are still the fastest growing institutions of higher education in America. Yet whatever degree of success they may have achieved, they are still regarded widely as poor step-children, as even the term "junior college" suggests.

If education is to serve human needs, and if institutions devoted especially to the education of women are to serve women especially and meet *their* needs as distinctive persons and not second-class males, then present time patterns need to be challenged.

Why? Because there are some basic facts of life which are now commonly ignored.

First of all, no matter how much educators may decry it or how much cajoling may be done to modify it, girls are simply not prepared to take as long getting a formal education as men. Of the best high school graduates who go on to college only 37 per cent of the women complete four years of college as compared to 55 per cent of the men. More than half of all women who enter college never complete a baccalaureate degree.

The average age of first marriage for women is just under 20 years. The age has been going down steadily since 1890, when it was 22. According to Sutherland, this is not only the youngest age in this country, but it is the youngest for all countries of the Western world.[1]

Except to overly ambitious parents or to the professor who can see nothing but the book in front of his nose, this should not be surprising. For the dice of our society in this part of the 20th century are certainly loaded.

Women are also having their families earlier than ever. In 1890 the average woman had her last child at 32; in 1957 the age was 26. If they aren't having children, married women are working—helping their husbands through college and graduate school or supplementing the usually inadequate income of early career years.

Add to these statistics the fact that large segments of our society have never really been convinced that a college education is terribly central in the development of a woman. After all, they argue, what does knowledge of Bohr's law or Kant's categorical imperative add to the capacity to change a diaper?

A young woman accordingly faces an almost irresistable series of pressures—the pressure of the peer group that suggests she's missed the boat if she isn't engaged by 20, the pressure of families to "do something useful" before she gets married, the pressure to have a marketable skill apart from being a woman, plus the fact that there is no consistent and impelling supportive pressure to assure her that college is really worthwhile.

To assume that American colleges and universities can forever attempt to fly in the face of such pressures is naive. "If you can't fight 'em, join 'em" has been advice useful in other settings. Perhaps it's applicable to education. It would not be unwarranted compromising nor too easy capitulation to forces outside of education to suggest that we begin patterning higher education of women to recognize these facts.

In the interest of respecting the integrity of women as persons, women's colleges, at least, should abandon the time stereotypes in which we now seem trapped and develop new patterns which are more nearly feminine, or rather which more realistically meet women's distinctive needs.

More specifically, women's colleges should deliberately move toward abandoning the typical two-year or four-year patterns and develop instead multi-degree programs to be completed in different periods of time in the same institutions.

In the woman's college of the future legitimate programs of study might be completed in two, three, four, or five years with appropriate degrees conferred to honor the work completed. Because large numbers of girls are prepared for many reasons to devote no more than two years to formal education, the most creative programs possible would be developed for this two-year span; and at the end, instead of leaving the two-year student with a sense of defeat and failure as is now the case with such a girl in the four-year college, an appropriate degree would be offered to signify the completion of a job well done. (The Associate of Arts degree now offered by junior colleges is already acceptable for this.)

For the committed student who wants more than a minimum two years, yet who is reluctant to give four years of her young life to education, accelerated three-year degrees can be developed which make more intensive use of a student's time. Already there is a considerable uneasiness among young women in devoting their summers to loafing at beaches or pools or participating in contrived but non-productive activity. Programs which make deliberate and maximum use of summers combined with slightly more than average effort during the normal academic year can legitimately lead to the awarding of bachelor's degrees at the end of the third year.

The more traditional programs can be provided for those who like the relative leisure of the present four-year baccalaureate degree programs.

I assume also that the really strong institutions have competent staffs which would enable offering work beyond the normal bachelor's degree—at least in a few fields. By more imaginative planning of the interrelationship of the normal undergraduate program with the first stage of graduate work, more creative and useful programs could be developed leading to the Master of Arts degree at the end of five years for teaching or other specialities. Institutions would need to be selective in identifying these advanced fields in which they propose to work, but most could do something.

Further variations in time would be provided if we remember that students learn at different speeds and basically have different competencies. By taking cognizance of this, still other time patterns may emerge.

Actually there is nothing very radical in this proposal, for by one device or another in many university systems, something comparable to this is possible. I am only proposing that what happens by accident and default in other places should be deliberately adopted as policy by the imaginative woman's college. Thus, instead of typing colleges as two-year or four-year, junior or senior, we should strike an emancipating blow for a distinctively woman's college which refuses to be classified by time but insists upon its identity as a college for women—

with all of the flexibility in programs, degrees, and time spans which the distinctive needs of women suggest.

If we are to maintain the integrity of women as persons, we must also challenge a second assumption that the formal education of women should be confined to and completed within the age range of 17 to 21. This is another hoax which has been perpetrated on women by a male-dominated society.

Such a pattern may be good for the male, who must get as much preparation as early in his career as possible so he can move promptly into his work well prepared and continue without important inter-ruption for further preparation. Thus his professional or business progress is not impeded while he works uninterruptedly to produce the ulcer or coronary which will eventually kill him.

A woman's life is seldom such a pell-mell and uninterrupted plunge down a single-tracked path. College leads to work or marriage or both. When marriage comes, if it does come, it is no mere incident, temporarily distracting from some other career. For most it is life's major event, "not to be entered into lightly or unadvisedly," and it calls for a major effort. There is work in and out of the home, and children with running noses, and house work and fights with neighbor's children, and adolescent problems. And mothers, bless them, do something about all these things.

But children grow up and move away from home, and husbands finally find their niche where the efforts of even the most ambitious wives must settle into a supportive role, and life at 40 or 45 stretches on for what may be long years of early retirement from activity which demanded all her energies and gave meaning to her life.

It is unrealistic to suppose that a woman can prepare for the multiplicity of roles and the dichotomies which mark important turn-ing points in her life by any single educational experience confined to late adolescence, no matter how creative or fundamental it may be. Advocates of the liberal arts will not like this, for the liberally educated person should be prepared to cope with any of life's exigencies, the argument goes. Yet as a graduate of a traditional liberal arts college and of one of the most traditional graduate schools of the country, I would argue that this is wishful thinking, even if I am not a woman.

In life's early preparatory years in college we can at best help pre-pare young women for the years immediately ahead which can be imaginatively reproduced and anticipated—and this seldom includes the dark unknown of the years of 39 and on. And we can hope to kindle the interest in and capacity for self-stimulated learning which may carry on throughout life. But the latter is again largely wishful academic dreaming, if we can judge by careful studies of the intellectual growth patterns of the average college graduate.

This leads me to conclude that, for the good of society and of women as persons, colleges devoted to the education of women must extend their concern beyond the period of late adolescence and develop programs which reach out to meet the needs of women of more mature years.

There are two illustrations of what might be done in this area. First, women's colleges could do much to promote the extension of continuing intellectual and cultural growth through informal avenues open through alumnae clubs and *ad hoc* groups of college graduates. It is not hard to believe that considerable numbers of women would be willing to give up a ceaseless round of meetings on flower arranging, a trip to the shrines of Virginia, or scholarship drives for the college (important as the latter might be to a college president) in favor of some serious intellectual fare designed to meet a variety of previously unmet needs. I have been impressed, for example, with the response to a body of material on the humanities made available to alumnae groups by the Stephens College program. And some experiments among groups of alumnae clubs in certain metropolitan centers have made available solid intellectual meat on which large numbers have been chewing.

But I am even more sanguine about the contribution which could be made by work which could be offered on women's college campuses designed especially for the mature young woman of 39 and over, whose family has passed from the home and who is now seeking to get a second wind for the latter half of life.

Industry has developed a vast array of courses for its promising younger as well as older personnel. They range from the most practical to the most esoteric and they are held in factory cafeterias in New York or plush mountain retreats in Colorado. In these programs of on-the-job training and widening of intellectual horizons of key personnel, industry is currently investing unbelievable sums of money. By and large American industry does not operate as a philanthropic enterprise, and it is obvious it expects an important return on this investment.

If industry is convinced that supplementation of training serves important ends, is it too far fetched to assume that supplementary further education of mature women may also serve important ends in our society. I am prepared to argue that one of the greatest unused and undeveloped potentials for good in American society is the still young, mature woman of 39 and over.

These are women to whom colleges concerned about women's education should be giving some attention. As a minimum they should be developing summer programs, at least as attractive as seminars for executives established by industry, to provide two-, four-, or six-week seminar experience for women.

Programs could be developed to stimulate again the intellectual enterprise which may have been thwarted and submerged during years of changing diapers and wiping running noses; to explore new areas of cultural and social interests for which there may never have been time in hurried adolescence or since; to develop leadership for community responsibility; to open new careers for later years. Possibilities are limited only by the imagination and resources of the colleges. There is, of course, no reason to confine this to summers but this might be at least a starting point.

The third assumption which needs to be challenged is that colleges must be devoted exclusively to things of the mind.

Now before anyone accuses me of being anti-intellectual or suggests I am proposing to substitute a Slenderella routine for the rigors of a more serious academic discipline, let me hasten to explain.

The fundamental raison d'etre for a college or university in our society is, of course, to cultivate the intellectual virtues. We live in a luxury culture where it is not necessary for every girl to begin to contribute to the common good by manual labor as soon as she is able to swing a broom. To the contrary, we can afford as a society to delay entrance into productive work for a considerable period. Accordingly our society, believing that the development of brain power can contribute to the individual's and its long-range good, sets aside institutions in which this development can take place. And it frees young people from other responsibilities so that they may in these institutions seek to realize more fully their potential. Any college or university which fails to fulfill to the best of its ability the fundamental intellectual task for which it has been set aside and allowed to exist is failing both the society and the students who have placed their destinies in its lap.

Having taken a stand against compromising the basic role of a college, may I repeat the earlier challenge that colleges need not and ought not to be devoted exclusively to things of the mind. There is no moral or historical ground for suggesting that colleges cannot and should not deliberately do much more than this minimum job.

It is not a "brain" or "mind" alone that goes to college. A whole human being goes. At the other end of the line, when a mature woman is employed or married, it is not merely a brain with legs and arms which enters into a relationship but a whole human personality.

The great traditional schools and universities abroad have been proud of the plus quality in their training. The English brag of the leaders of the empire who have been fashioned on the playing fields of Eton or forged into gentlemen in the commons rooms of colleges in Cambridge or Oxford. Yale and Harvard are proud of the character of their men moulded by traditions built up over scores of student generations. And at Washington and Lee a man is always a gentleman no matter what else.

Women's institutions, however, have been defensive and sensitive, especially in more recent years, when it has been suggested that their contribution to a woman may be more than academic. This defensiveness is understandable in light of the struggle to establish women's colleges as something more than female seminaries or finishing schools. This battle has been effectively won, yet the better women's colleges have become uncompromising bastians of academic exclusiveness seeking to camouflage every other feminine virtue.

Haven't we achieved the kind of maturity now which makes it possible once more to acknowledge openly that a college is seriously concerned about a woman as a person as well as a brain; that college is an appropriate place to continue to develop the whole range of basic competencies which are called for in the life of a woman?

To take this seriously will mean that the curriculum will be affected. It will need to take account of the fact that women do lead lives with different patterns than men, approach common problems from different perspectives, and have need of special areas of knowledge.

It also means we have to take a different view of the opportunities for growth which are available in the out-of-class activity of a college. Currently the quickest way to get an educational article published in a popular magazine or to organize a rally of professors is to take some good jabs at extra-curricular activities. It's good indoor academic sport to belabor panty raids, hunkering, gold-fish eating, or whatever happens to be the current faddist obsession. Yet it is not only these extremes but *every activity* not related to a lecture or books which get in the way of good student academic performance, some argue. At best, they continue, the organized clubs, student government, student union activities are to be tolerated as inevitable outbursts of adolescent enthusiasm to be curbed by regulation and kept to a minimum and properly policed.

To take this attitude is to ignore some of the greatest opportunities for constructive contribution to the maturing of a person available anywhere in our society. College contributes importantly to personal development beyond intellectual dimensions. Learning to relate in a mature way to peers and to elders, developing capacities for leadership and constructive group activity, achieving high standards for personal and group living, finding a meaningful religious orientation for life are not inconsequential matters. Adequate counselling resources, purposeful student activity programs, and the deliberate cultivation of a campus climate supporting high ideals in personal and group affairs can make a difference. To change from a policy of policing to a policy of maximizing these additional learning opportunities could bring radical changes in students.

To take this more positive approach seriously means:

1. Believing in the wholeness of persons, that segments of persons— including minds—cannot be isolated, and the whole of a human being is worth developing.

2. Investing in professional leadership. Maximum learning opportunities in dormitories, dining halls or playing fields, in club meetings and student government or publications will not happen by chance any more than disciplined learning in mathematics happens by chance. Trained leadership is essential to assist in structuring learning opportunities and taking advantage of "teachable moments."

3. Relinquishing the notion that the classroom is the only place on campus where important learning takes place.

4. A willingness to make time available for this kind of learning.

The constructive program which can emerge from all this will take seriously the importance of women as persons and will produce more able and more interesting women.

4

DEVELOPING INTELLECTUAL CURIOSITY

GRELLET C. SIMPSON

Real education—intellectual education—is not the total growth and development of an individual, but the kind of education for which schools and colleges are created to make available to those who have the ability and the spunk to develop their talents.

This is not to imply that one's total being should go undernourished, unloved, or forgotten, but simply that schools and colleges exist to do a job that other agencies should not be able to do better, and the schools and colleges should not undertake to do a much larger job that other institutions of our society should and could do better.

I am, of course, referring to colleges whose major responsibility is to develop the intellectual capacity of their students—and I make no exception to this position or responsibility if a college by chance limits its enrollment to women or to men.

Aware of my own attitude toward colleges and college students, I recalled a paragraph by a Mr. John Brown in McGuffey's *Sixth Eclectic Reader:*

"'Pray, Mr. Opie, may I ask you what you mix your colors with?' said a brisk dilettante student to the great painter. 'With brains, sir,' was the gruff reply—and the right one. It did not give much of information; it did not expound the principles and rules of art; but, if the inquirer had the commodity referred to, it would awaken him; it would set him agoing, athinking, and a-painting to good purpose. If he had not the wherewithal, as was likely enough, the less he had to do with colors and their mixture the better."[1]

As a first proposition, I suggest that Mr. Brown's definition of the primary "wherewithal" or "commodity" for the painter has a very uncomfortable relevance for all of us when we become concerned about our own lapses in intellectual curiosity—not only for the *"now"* but for the *"future."* However, I doubt that we can blame society or fate whenever we fall from intellectual grace. We really can blame only ourselves, since continuing intellectual curiosity is essentially the result of a very definite act of the will of the individual—making a practice of using one's own brain, as the artist suggests, rather than relying on others to do our thinking for us while our own minds only nibble at the edges of thought. It is not extra time or extra energies or "change of environment" that is needed to motivate the will to act in one's behalf, but rather self-determination and continuous practice in the art of thinking.

My second proposition is related to a very ancient concept in medieval law—the idea of *obedience to the unenforceable*. I cannot put this concept into the social, political, or religious context of its original creation, nor can I trace its evolution in later legal history. But I am convinced that its application to our intellectual development has been, and will continue to be, the greatest motivating factor in the intellectual maturity and achievements of the truly great, or near-great, throughout all ages.

All of us know what is meant by the term *law*, or rule, and obedience thereto, but are we always conscious of the even more imperative demand for obedience to an *absence* of enforceable rule, without which it is impossible to attain and retain that true sense of order which motivates genuine intellectual curiosity? One's education is valid only if he finds himself ready to live in the dual world of these two obediences.

No one can *make* us think. Sound education encourages and stimulates a person to think, but oftentimes the motivation is based on the momentary incentive rather than upon the value inherent in the thinking process itself. If learning is pursued wisely, one accepts the intellectual value of thinking as a possible end in itself, and not just a means—hopefully present when needed—of getting "over the hump" for the time being. An "intellectual laggard," then, is the person who does not possess sufficient will or desire to be obedient to a power which is a uniquely human attribute—the power to think, which is the result of constant discipline, constant use, and a continuing obedience to the unenforceable.

Pascal wrote that "man is but a reed, the most feeble thing in nature, but he is a *thinking* reed."[2] While it is obedience to the unenforceable power to think that motivates genuine intellectual curiosity to a considerable extent, it is likewise this magic power of thinking that has given man, the feeble reed, the ability and the desire to weave all the threads of his existence into an overall pattern of intellectual solidarity and purposefulness, as he consciously strives to guide the shuttle of Truth through the warp and weft of everyday experience toward the attainment of man's innate worth and dignity.

What snares, what knots in the thread of man's thinking interfere with the development of his intellectual capacity? My third proposition, drawn from an interpretation of a short passage in the *Novum Organum* of Francis Bacon, suggests the answer. The intellectual achievement of our civilization, Bacon says, is "like the branches of a tree that meet in one stem." [3] The establishment of man's empire over nature depends upon intellectual solidarity—*the stem of the tree*— which, in turn, is nurtured by the roots of intellectual curiosity. The lopped-off branch, the withered limb, the diseased leaf, and the spoiled fruit are results of damage to the stem—not the cause of it. Therefore, what caused the stem to become damaged concerned Bacon greatly— as it should all of us.

Bacon was bothered by what he termed "mental idols"—the fallacies and errors which mislead the mind and cause man to go astray in his thinking. What are these idols, these fallacies, that entangle our thinking? What are these imperfect patterns of growth that sap the vitality of the main stem of human understanding, and which we must constantly try to avoid with all possible care?

First is the "idol of the tribe," inherent in the race of man itself. It is man's tendency to assert that the standard of things is determined by the thinking or conclusions of the group, ignoring the fact that the threads of human thinking often become knotted and twisted in an effort to follow the group pattern. Two minds are not necessarily better than one *thinking* mind. However, two *thinking* minds are always better than one, for that means the fallacy of the tribe, the group, the clique, can be avoided. We have only to read the papers or listen to an average conversation or discussion to realize that the fallacy of the tribe often dominates and controls the life and the thought of the individual, sometimes without justification and without reason.

This does not mean that groups or tribes have not arrived at truths to which they rightly cling with fervor and conviction. Yet, to avoid the possibility that the group itself may be following a pattern no longer useful—a twisting of the facts to make them conform to outmoded dogma or customs which actually have no basis in truth—society must insure for the individual his right to suggest a different pattern, and for us our privilege to listen to his suggestion.

No one in our free nation would deny any man his right to speak, but to avoid the possible fallacy of the tribe, we must *listen*—with our minds; we must think things through to logical and realistic conclusions. We must not accept the opinion of the group simply because it *is* the opinion of the group, and we should decide for ourselves whether or not we can honestly agree with the view of the tribe.

Just as there are fallacies of the group, there are likewise fallacies of the individual—the "idol of the den," as Bacon says. Everyone has his own personal faculties which stretch the warp or tangle the weft, arising from his own disposition or from his education and association with others, or from his reading or the authority over him acquired by those he respects and admires, or from a different pattern impressed on the mind, as it happens to be preoccupied and prejudiced, or undisturbed and tranquil. The result is variable, often confused, and seemingly at times actuated by chance.

This fallacy is most frequently demonstrated by what the non-academic world calls scornfully the "ivory tower" of the teacher, the scholar, the recluse. I wonder why the work-a-day world feels that schoolteachers (eggheads, rather) have a monopoly on these ivory towers. Has it ever occurred to them that each facet of society has its own ivory towers—each essentially bad? Man in any walk of life may build his ideas, his job, his business, his profession, his home, his family, his club, even his church, into an ivory tower. The redeeming factor, the escape from this fallacy of the individual, is the knowledge that in a free society ivory towers need never exist. When they do, they are man's error, not predestined patterns to which all must conform. And man's escape from this fallacy is dependent upon his guarding against not so much the other fellow's ivory tower as his own. The difficulty, of course, lies in the fact that it is so much easier for one to point out the other fellow's tower than it is to see that there might just as readily be a very privileged "tower" in his own mental attic—or cellar.

I remember the lines:

"The fault, dear Brutus, is not in our stars But in ourselves, that we are underlings." [4]

The third idol or fallacy Bacon calls the 'idol of the market." I might risk bowing down to this idol in presenting some ideas bearing a great educational significance. The fallacy arises with all those with whom we come in contact; it involves primarily communication, for language is the universal means of communication. The meaning of words is dependent upon the understanding of the person who uses them, as well as the understanding of the person who hears them, and is controlled only in part by dictionary definitions. The "error of the market place," or idol of communication, arises from a bad or unwise choice of words and creates an amazing obstruction to the mind. Words unmistakably force the understanding, are capable of throwing everything into confusion, and frequently lead people into vain and unnecessary controversies.

We grapple with this idol as we try to read an insurance policy, complete an income tax form, express an idea in words—not just merely to state a fact, make a talk that seeks to stimulate a discussion of ideas rather than to answer a simple question or propound a specific view on a given topic. I have endeavored to force an understanding of some of the fallacies that the *thinking* person needs to guard against in order to develop his intellectual curiosity to the fullest extent. Have I succeeded, or will some persons be convinced that I meant one thing, when I am equally confident that I meant another?

Finally, the fallacy of dogma, or as Bacon calls it, the "idol of the theatre" must concern us. Bacon viewed this fallacy, resulting from the systems of philosophy (political or otherwise) then known or yet to be stated, as so many plays brought out and performed, thereby creating a factitious and theatrical world. He was primarily concerned, and so should we all be, with those general systems of thought established by tradition and unquestioning acceptance, and at times maintained by neglect.

I should like to approach this point by asking a few questions: What is democracy? Do we believe in it? What is liberal education? Do we really know? What is free enterprise? Are we in favor of it? What is capitalism? Can we define it?

Now on the contrary side of the picture: What is socialism? Does it creep? What is a radical? Is he fundamentally bad? What is communism? Do we know *why* we are against it?

By these questions I suggest that we at times allow the fallacy of dogma to exist in order to dodge the honest investigation into truth. All our thinking is inevitably encircled by numerous frames of reference or set patterns of belief, and we constantly get our wires crossed. We need a greater awareness that wires do get crossed, that oftentimes in our thinking we do "blow a fuse."

To develop intellectual curiosity now and for the future, one should be constantly vigilant lest he fall victim to the fallacies discerned by Francis Bacon. For whenever he does, the precise and well-developed power of thought which best motivates mankind to enjoy and profit from the use of his mind is thereby curtailed. I submit all education should lead to this fully disciplined intellectual life. If we continue to maintain this goal of the academic years on into the fuller years of adult maturity, we need hardly worry about isolated bodies of subject matter so easily obtainable when we need to know them. We have too often assumed that mere acquaintance with bodies of fact will motivate the mind to think.

My fourth proposition is, therefore, that the most infallible motivation for continuing intellectual curiosity is based more upon acquiring the conviction of the essential beauty of Truth, as perceived by the fully disciplined mind to explore all knowledge, than it is upon the idea that this continuing intellectual curiosity is dependent upon momentary interests, tested aptitudes, personality quotients, and social adaptability.

I should like to suggest what I see as the ultimate goal of man as he moves in his moment of opportunity through life. In the truest sense, our civilization will find its fulfillment only in the intellectual and moral solidarity of our inheritors. Our moral life is dependent for its maturity on the truly intellectually disciplined curiosity which today, and for all days, we wish so hopefully to engender. We need constantly to remind ourselves that this peace, this solidarity, this fulfillment, will not be passed on to our inheritors except through the turmoil and the hope, the pain and the joy, the sorrow and the exaltation, through which we make our lives the artistic creations for which purpose our Creator has given us our minds.

As James Joyce, in writing *A Portrait of the Artist as a Young Man*,[5] is the mature artist, so Stephen, the hero, is a representation of the artist-by-nature as he discovers his vocation, defines his creed, and sets forth to practice it. Stephen's life happened to him as everyone's life happens, at all hours and seasons, any old way, with a kind of chronic inconvenience. So it is with most of us, and yet we read with interest and profit of Stephen's existence, presented in rich detail by Joyce in a fashion of deliberate and conscious artistic composition.

Stephen tries to find himself through obedience, through disobedience, through his family, through dreams, through friends or an absence of them, through precocious sensuality, through intellectual speculations, and finally, and most earnestly, through rigorous piety. Each and every attempt fails, or seems to fail. He only learns in recurrent weariness and despair that he is not *this*, not *that*. Then suddenly, after he has resisted the temptation to be trapped by vanity into entering a vocation for which he is not suited, Freedom possesses him, *Freedom and Expectation.* He wanders out onto the strand at the north side of the river mouth where presentiment has long since warned him he would meet his love and all the loveliness of living which the young woman symbolizes.

Bond after bond falls away from him; weariness is banished. Joyfully he welcomes his final separation from all that does not truly and wholly pertain to himself. He knows with absolute certainty that he is approaching his destiny in the "wild heart of life." Thus, the Stephen-Joyce sequence of Freedom and Expectation—loveliness—and finally, destiny in the "wild heart of life."

With this sequence of experiences Joyce characterizes what I call Stephen's awakening—intellectually, morally, even spiritually.

All of us can recall certain moments of startling realization, which Joyce in a letter referred to as Freedom and Expectation. The "wild heart of life," is different for all people who choose to cultivate their differing talents. Otherwise it would not be life in general, have a heart, or be in any sense "wild" or natural.

To me, the "wild heart of life" is able to laugh with joy, with sorrow, with anger, even with remorse. In these days of angry young men and women, the "wild heart of life" looks back *not* with anger or self-pity, but rather with the touch of the poet who sees beyond himself, and looks with compassionate laughter *at* himself. Neither Stephen nor any of us can capture Joyce's goal for life if we do not recapture a comic spirit that will bring sanity, perspective, and unsparing self-appraisal once more into our daily lives. We are afraid to laugh because others moan; we are terrified that we will be laughed *at* because we have failed to fit some mass formula of living that actually no one can prescribe for anyone else or even for himself.

There is no freedom of the mind or soul without the comic spirit, and there can be no expectation of the "loveliness" of Joyce in our "wild heart of life" when it is smothered, when its existence is denied. Likewise, the "wild heart of life" expands as life expands, and its loveliness increases.

Above all else, the "wild heart of life" *thinks* as no mind alone can think. The "thinking heart" is a man's noblest attainment. With it he lives more profoundly, more creatively, more joyously on this planet. The "thinking heart" of Beethoven was able to shout "Freude!" when the mind or the heart alone could only sigh in bitter resignation. Great tragedy, great comedy, great poetry, great painting, great ideas are the product of the "thinking heart." However, the heart must be trained and disciplined to think; it can *function* without thought. Likewise, the mind can *think* without a heart, but it cannot think joyously. The "thinking heart" is in truth the means of our earthly glory and assuredly the basis of hope for any spiritual consolation.

Stephen's "wild heart of life" thus laughs, expands, and thinks. But to what purpose? To what end? In my opinion, Sean O'Casey gives the answer in his play *Within the Gates,* where the Dreamer (he could be called Stephen) speaks prophetically: "No one has a right to life who doesn't fight to make it greater. I shall follow after loveliness all the days of my life."[6]

The "wild heart of life" is attainable for all of us if we "follow after loveliness" (or Truth) "all the days of (our) lives." This loveliness to which both Joyce and O'Casey refer is not unlike the platonic idea of earlier writers, who called it by various names: by one, *sapientia* (or wisdom), by another, *intellectual beauty.* It is the grand intellectual achievement that Francis Bacon envisioned for the man who is able to resist those mental idols which he so deftly exposes in his *Novum Organum;* or, it is that quality of mind that Petronius found so endearing in the poet, Horace, when he spoke of his "curiosa felicitas."[7] But I prefer to call it the "wild heart of life," which laughs, which expands and grows, which thinks, not merely because, or when, it wishes to do so, but by an inexorable dedication of the will to become obedient to that which is unenforceable—in the restlessness, at times in the turbulence, but most often in the sheer joy that emanates from the man who has truly developed and utilized his intellectual curiosity "all the days of (his) life."

TOWARD SUCCESSFUL FAMILY LIVING

EDNA P. AMIDON

Most individuals spend their lives in a family; they marry and have children, and it is in their homes that children begin to learn to be cooperative, sensitive to the needs of others, and systematic in their approach to problems; or conversely, to be antagonistic, selfish, opinionated. Colleges have an obligation to help prepare women for exercising leadership in maintaining the highest quality of home and family living.

How can this obligation be carried out? In very general terms, colleges should give their women students the following as a basis for exercising this leadership:

1. A realization of how woman's role has changed in this day of combining family and career.

2. An understanding of how far-reaching the influences of the family are, and that, therefore, family life matters, and matters a great deal.

3. A realization that the way in which a woman organizes her life is related to, in fact is an expression of, her philosophy of living.

4. An understanding of human growth and development so that she will be able to respect the differences between human beings, both in the home and in the community; to help rather than hinder others in their search for self-fulfillment; and to be aware of her own needs in the different stages of her life.

5. An understanding of the physical sciences, which gives her a respect for "cause and effect" in everyday happenings in the home and community.

6. A knowledge about the economic forces in our society—how they affect her life and how, as a consumer and citizen, she registers her approval or disapproval and thus influences what is made available to her family in goods and services through both private and public channels.

7. An awareness of the beautiful and the ability to express it in her

choices so that whatever she does, whether with mind, heart, or hand, expresses her feeling for beauty.

8. The kind of understanding of history and cultures that helps her give her children a feeling for the responsibilities of citizens, and an understanding of the sources of prejudice and the need for cooperative effort in the solution of world problems.

9. A realization that interdisciplinary research is helping to solve home and family problems, and that this research is increasing and is of great importance for the future.

10. A knowledge of the kinds of abilities she needs if she is to foster a successful family in this technological age, and an understanding that through systematic study she can develop these abilities and so be freed to express her creativity in daily life.

In discussing how a college is to provide this equipment, three questions must be answered:

One, are there new conditions in our world today that make education of wives and mothers for successful family life a subject requiring organized study at the college level?

Two, should one propose an education for women as wives and mothers instead of education for a professional career or general education available to all women?

Three, can one discuss the subject out of reference to the requirements of men's education?

My position is (1) that unique conditions today require, as a part of woman's education, preparation for leadership in family life as wife and mother; (2) that this education is over and above, but still a part of, her general education and an important supplement to her professional education; and (3) that the colleges must find a way to provide this kind of education.

In answer to the third question, men as well as women need in their college education today certain basic understandings about the family—its importance in our society and its potential for personal fulfillment; they need to understand the responsibilities of adults for a high quality of family life and what is at stake in failing to prepare adequately for it. How this shall be provided for men is not a part of the assignment, but men are enrolling in almost equal numbers with women in college courses in marriage and the family where they are offered. And the number of such offerings is on the increase.

Change is very much with us and its rate will be accelerated. Changing conditions affect family life and call for new abilities, attitudes, and understandings.

From the beginning of life in this country the home has been recognized as a fundamental character-building institution, and parents have been generally held—in the eyes of neighbors at least—responsible for the behavior of their children. Traditional patterns of mother-daughter and father-son relationships have been passed on from one generation to the next.

Young couples had in the past little or no choice in deciding how to live; their houses were much the same as their parents', as were their furnishings, their equipment, and their food. People lived in one community all their lives and among neighbors who knew a great deal about them. This now has changed. The traditional pattern of life no longer prevails for a great majority of our people; for many young couples there is likely to be no "set pattern" of home living that they need to follow. Young people with unlike cultural backgrounds face many real conflicts when they establish their own homes, for choices are possible that were never possible before. To choose means to exercise judgment, and the development of ability to make sound judgments is a most difficult educational task. Life has become complex in every area.

Along with social, economic, and technological developments have come improvements in our material standards of living, an increase in the proportion of children and youth seeking more education, and new knowledge in human relationships. There also has come, at least for some people, a high expectation for a satisfying marriage and family life.

As technological and social changes open up new opportunities for women's careers, the college educated woman looks more and more on part of her college education as preparation for a profession. And for an increasing number the basic decision is not whether to pursue a career, but how to dovetail marriage, motherhood, and community responsibility with a profession or professional work.

Today our shrinking world often requires people from widely different cultures to work with others in the solution of complex problems. New knowledge, new demands, and new horizons call for the kind of family leadership that makes the home not only a place in which adults can find security, human understanding, and creative outlets essential in a world grown tense with its complexities, but a place in which its individual members are given an opportunity to develop to their fullest capacities.

The husband and wife teamwork approach to home responsibilities is a growing and wholesome trend among young couples. Nevertheless, the wife's and mother's role—in her own expectations and for all practical purposes—still requires that she be in "command" as far as the over-all direction of home responsibilities is concerned. In the disorganized home operated without knowledge or skill, there is little opportunity for truly creative experience. The young mother who lacks basic knowledge of infant development and home management, who is unacquainted with all the resources available for the home nowadays—new products, new equipment, new kinds of credit, new communities—finds herself frequently so frustrated by failures that she is totally incapable of making the kind of home that is for her family a haven from the tensions of the outside world.

That many families are having difficulty in making the adjustment to the rapidly changing conditions of our society is evident on every side. A preliminary summary of the States' reports of problems for consideration by the 1960 White House Conference on Children and Youth indicated that problems of family relationship ranked high among those mentioned.

Our mental hospitals are crowded; the number of children in broken homes continues to increase daily. Clearly, many professional and community services are needed to serve our growing population, but where are we going to get these services? Surely, competent young women must be urged to provide them, either for money or for the joy of service.

Therefore we must provide an education that will prepare young women to combine marriage and parenthood with careers and community service.

Our challenge, then, is to make education for woman's role as a wife and mother in successful family life, an essential part of her college education. Adequately conceived and carried out, it will enable her (1) to carry her share of responsibility for providing a home environment in which all members of the family can achieve their greatest potential; (2) to multiply her own opportunities, both within and outside the family, for self-realization; (3) to make more effective her contributions as a citizen; and (4) to increase the number of ways in which she and the other members of her family can make a contribution to the work of a broader world. Certainly, above all, we must remember that no one enjoys a responsibility unless she feels competent to carry it.

The equipment listed earlier, which the college can give its women students, indicates contributions from many basic disciplines that are interrelated and need to be applied to life today. Unfortunately, we do not have much successful experience in helping students to integrate what they learn from the different disciplines. Here is where we need to explore and experiment with the "how." I have three general suggestions.

First, how can we give students some help in seeing the importance and scope of this goal early in their college years? It seems to me that all students need help in realizing the importance of the family in our society and in becoming aware of how change is affecting American family life. In addition, each student needs insight into the overall functions of the home in providing continuity in our culture—preserving what should not be lost from the old order while we evolve the new, and in creating for her family, separated by distance and a new concept of independence from the older generation, the security that young families once drew from their forebears in a less mobile and more stable world. Probably most of all she needs to realize that growth toward a healthy emotional maturity is an essential characteristic in good husband-wife relationships. Such a focus on family living is also needed to give women perspective in meeting their immediate problems and to prepare them for later stages in their lives. As the college works toward these goals, the students can be helped to see that answers come from many areas of learning.

In a growing number of colleges and universities, offerings are now being provided through courses or seminars which focus on the family and which aim at helping students achieve some of the goals just mentioned. Evaluation of such courses indicates that through them students gain insights which they themselves consider to be of immediate personal value and which they apply in married life after college. There is an accumulation of experience among colleges and universities throughout the United States in making these study opportunities interdepartmental, with staff from various disciplines contributing to the courses.

The need for college students to have first-hand contact with pertinent problems facing women is being met in a variety of ways.

One university uses a simple plan for freshmen students in home economics enrolled in a course on "The Changing Role of Women and the Implications for Education" to gain insight into some of the practical problems being faced by homemakers in relation to work outside the home, and to bring reality into their class discussions. These students interview working mothers. Such provocative remarks from the interviews as these are brought back to class for discussion: "Oh, my mother takes care of the children; I have important work to do in my professional field!" and "We can get so many more things for the children when I work."[1]

How the husband's role changes with the wife's is suggested, too, as these students interview husbands of working wives. Such interesting variations in reactions as these are expressed: "When she has a job I feel that I simply must help with the household chores and take more time with the children. I can't keep on doing this and still keep up with my competitors." "Of course . . . it's sometimes mighty inconvenient for all of us when my wife takes special courses and goes to summer school, but we think it's a good 'life insurance'. I will feel a whole lot better when I know she can hold a good job in case anything ever happens to me."

My second suggestion calls for a faculty committed to education for family life as a worthy goal and willing to help students focus their learnings on the problems of the family. A woman's college that is serious about achieving the goal of preparing its students as wives and mothers will need faculty members in sympathy with this goal.

Commitment to focusing learnings on family problems presents many obstacles. In some instances it will call for a team approach not easy to achieve at a time of increasing enrollment because it takes time. Also, many specialists do not see the relationship of their subject to living problems; they may consider any effort to help students see the relationship a waste of their efforts, and in some respects implying a lack of intelligence on the part of students who do not see the relationship.

Very few students, for example, achieve the kind of understanding of the physical sciences which gives them a respect for "cause and effect" in everyday happenings in the home and community; for most students it is gained only as they are provided with experience in tracing these "cause and effect" relationships in the solution of the kinds of problems with which they are familiar.

Foster and Wilson, in their book on *Women After College,* tell of a class of 30 women, all of whom had passed, with good grades, college inorganic and organic chemistry and physics; they were asked to give six examples of the application of chemistry and physics to household management. "As simple as this might seem to the professor of chemistry or physics," the authors said, "not a single girl could give and discuss a single principle involved until they were given examples by the instructor, and then they could not give the principles involved." They go on to mention: "One method, reported by one woman, for partially overcoming this difficulty was a system of interdepartmental seminars organized around topics of practical interest and discussed by students from the physical, social, and biological sciences as well as from the fine arts."[2]

Probably it is only by first-hand experience in helping people solve real and important problems that specialists from two or more related fields can gain an understanding of how difficult and important this focusing of knowledge on everyday problems of living is, and how it frequently requires recognizing the contribution to be made from other fields of knowledge in the ultimate solution of a problem that superficially, at least, seems, for example, only an economic one or a biological one.

At a conference on infant development held in the Merrill-Palmer School in Detroit, I heard a report by a pediatrician and a psychiatrist on their teamwork. The respect each showed for the other's field and the way each was able to relate his own contribution to that of the other was inspiring. They said: "Our goal is to integrate what we know with what is practical; to try to overcome bias and habit as it grows out of each of our disciplines." They said this integration had been necessary because they had served in a consulting capacity to parents and "family problems do not come in the kind of categories in which we organize our knowledge."

My third suggestion is that colleges provide certain courses organized around special areas of home life. Dr. George Stoddard, in his small but comprehensive book *On the Education of Women,* recommended certain specific education which he called "home education." He wrote: "Everybody needs home education, although the woman will use it more than the man. It is rather late to undertake it at the time of marriage as a quick preparation for one's future life."[3] He raises the question as to how we can close the gap between knowledge and valid theory on the one hand, and insight at the level of practical application and decision-making on the other. The two suggestions I have already made will help to bridge this gap, but, in addition, *young women need experience in college in focusing on the study of basic home problems* organized around an area of family living. Here students learn to draw from many fields of study those principles which add to their understanding of home problems and ways of solving them. Furthermore, there is developing a body of knowledge based on research that draws for its techniques on the experience of the older sciences, but which is evolving its own research methods and results. The field of home economics is illustrative of this.

In discussing the need for more research in fields related to home and family life education, President C. A. Elvehjem of the University of Wisconsin speaks of home economics as the antidote to over-specialization.[4] The home economist in the role of teacher, or of student, is ideally situated to apply the findings of psychology, sociology, anthropology, biology, and many other specialties in a unified approach which draws on all contiguous disciplines.

In Dewey's theories of creative intelligence he defines the intelligence as "that behaviour or activity of the human organism in which a desired future is used to organize things, activities, ideas, instruments in such a way that the end is obtained."[5] This concept applied to the curriculum suggests that if an area of responsibility provides a unifying perspective, we can present knowledge from many fields in such a way that interrelations are seen. As curriculum builders, then, we should determine those areas of home or family responsibility which coincide with students' desired futures, and then find effective ways of providing education in these areas.

Colleges and universities are exploring a variety of ways of providing for all students courses that focus on home problems. Because of the limitation on students' time and the varying background of students, to date these courses have been more frequently offered as electives and have presented somewhat fragmentary approaches. Probably the most common practice has been to open to all students certain home economics courses such as nutrition, child development, family finance, textiles and clothing. My current thinking is that what is needed are courses or units of study provided especially for non-home economics majors, organized around areas of home responsibility basic to successful family living. These units would include nutrition, child development and growth, marriage and family relationships, home management, family housing, and possibly others.

One area of special study needed by college women is home management. To manage a home today calls for ability in dovetailing a wide variety of activities concerning care and education of the children, housekeeping, community responsibilities, and provisions for privacy of family members, for companionship between husband and wife, and for companionship of parents with children. This is the mere beginning of a list.

Physical surroundings are only one factor in management. The goals and objectives of the family have to be clear; there has to be agreement as to division of responsibility; the skills and special interests each family member has to contribute must be recognized; family members need to know the money, time, and energy that is available—all these factors must be considered.

A feeling of adequacy by the wife and mother in the planning and carrying out of plans is related to the family philosophy. The family has to reach some general agreements as to what standards can be maintained, which ones are most important, and how these can be safeguarded. The mother's poise and feeling of competence in carrying her responsibilities are dependent on such decisions.

Any serious study of home management today can draw on findings from research. Mrs. Gilbreth, a scientific engineer, early in this century began telling women how the principles of scientific management should and could be applied to the home. While business, industry, and agriculture have made rapid strides in the application of these principles, they have yet to be fully applied in the home, probably because women fear they might over-organize home life and ignore the individual family's needs and values. But these principles can be applied and are being applied with satisfaction by many women when the human elements in family living are given the high priority they deserve.

Dr. William W. McKee, head of undergraduate studies at the Merrill-Palmer School, has clarified for many people the importance of this high priority. He has shown the difference between "instrumental values" in home management (order, efficiency, skills, and planning), and the central *goal* value to which they contribute. He states the goal in these simple terms: " . . . home management seeks to create the conditions which will allow each person in the home to become the kind of person he is capable of becoming."

How are these conditions created? "They are created by each family as it makes a multitude of decisions in the day-to-day life of the family."⁵ Hence, ability in decision-making is of great importance. True, one can learn about ways to develop instruments for order, efficiency, etc., and can develop some skill in using them, but making decisions as to what is best for the individual family requires weighing many factors.

In the discussions of "Work in the Lives of Married Women," as carried on in the Arden House Conference in 1958, the individuality of families was recognized in such statements as these:

One cannot "generalize about families, about local communities or the nation as a whole, about socio-economic groups, about motives or attitudes."

" . . . there is no single problem which can be identified as 'the problem' of the working mother or wife," but rather we are dealing with "a complex of different and uneven problems, some of them major and others of trivial importance."

" . . . the same problem takes on different significance when viewed from different vantage points."⁷

There is a body of knowledge on which homemakers can draw in making home management decisions, but it is not readily available to them. The basic principles involved are drawn from many fields— from economics, psychology, physics, sociology, biology. To learn to make decisions that bring satisfaction to herself and to her family, a woman needs experience in defining a problem, getting the necessary facts about it, turning to research for knowledge of other significant data and for basic principles, and applying these to the solution of the problem. Through this experience she can come to recognize the interdependence of many facts and factors; she can gain ability in weighing these as they apply to real and specific situations; she can think through the consequences of alternative decisions; and she can discover practical ways to evaluate decisions made in different aspects of home life so that she will have better bases for future decisions.

Illustrations of the interrelatedness of factors involved in generalizing from this kind of study are implied in the following statements, which, though very simple, represent a welding of principles drawn from different fields.

"The stage of development of individual family members, as well as their special abilities, interests, and feelings, form the basis on which a satisfactory allocation of responsibilities rests."

"Management of the money, rather than the amount of the money, often determines the degree of solvency and the tensions that develop in families concerning money."

"Decisions regarding use of time and abilities are made more satisfactory when one assesses his resources accurately and projects his thinking to what the immediate and possible long-time effects of the decision will be upon personal growth and development of family members." Such ideas as these have meaning to students only as they are developed from experience, their own, supplemented by that of others and validated by what research is revealing.

Child development and family relationships illustrate two other areas of study of special significance to college women. During the last 30 years many colleges have included courses in child development, thus helping students achieve some understanding of themselves and some insights into how a child grows and develops. Except for majors in home economics and in elementary school teaching, such courses, however, have not been widely available to undergraduates. Some of this experience and some of the work being done for guidance counsellors and teachers in understanding adolescents should be drawn upon to help young women gain needed insight for the guidance of their own children.

Five points emphasized in well-guided education in child development were indicated by Dr. Gertrude Chittenden and Flo Gould after they had made a comprehensive examination of the literature and research findings in the field: (1) the role of the family in building personality; (2) the need to accept one's self and others as lovable; (3) the child's need for firm and consistent discipline; (4) the concept of the causality of behavior (a concept which, they point out, should be presented in its real complexity since no two individuals react in the same way to a situation); and (5) the idea that in democratic living each member is accepted for himself.[8]

John E. Anderson, writing on "The Development of Behavior and Personality," in the 1960 White House Conference on Children and Youth papers, summarizes his points quite effectively in the following paragraph:

"How then can we, in the broadest sense, characterize our desirable environment in relation to the early years? In our terms, it is one that is rich in the sense of stimulation, and supporting in the sense of affection. It is one that permits identification with models of desirable behavior. It is one that gives the child an opportunity to develop stable behavior patterns by not being erratic and inconsistent. It is one that enhances rather than degrades personality. In a phrase, it is one in which the primary concern is building up the child's confidence in his environment."[9]

To be effective for the prospective parent, education in child development requires that each student have the kind of experience with children which will put meaning into such content. The student needs to see a child over a continuous period of time to understand the interrelatedness of the child and his environment. Experiences with children have most frequently been provided in nursery schools, but more and more schools are finding additional ways for students to observe and know children of different ages in the home and community. Merrill-Palmer School has pioneered in exploring ways to provide students with experiences with children and youth. In planning a course to be provided as a part of the general education of all students, the faculty will need to study the practices of many institutions of learning in discovering and creating new ways of providing students with such experiences.

Many colleges and universities are providing special courses in marriage and family relationships which draw from many fields of study. In addition, there is developing from research a body of knowledge unique to this field.

Burgess and Wallin, in their book on *Engagement and Marriage,* "present," according to their preface, "the most extensive and intensive research yet made on courtship and the early years of marriage."[10] "Young people," they write, "confronted with change, uncertainty, and the increasing complexity of society realize that in the Atomic Age they cannot rely upon custom and common sense to solve their problems. They are, therefore," say the authors, "turning, in preparation for marriage, as for other life activities, to the knowledge derived from psychological and sociological research."[11]

Dr. Reuben Hill, Director of the Institute of the Family at the University of Minnesota, in an unpublished memorandum prepared for the Commissioner of the Social Security Administration, called attention to "certain interpersonal skills and competencies which family heads need to develop to exercise effectively family leadership . . . They partake of the peculiar properties of marriage and parent-child relations—the capacity to make one's self accessible to others, to handle intimate relationships, to serve others' needs, to understand one's self enough to relate self to others. The capacity to love and accept love, and the ability to sustain "intra-personal tensions engendered by conflicts, and resolve them; these are some of the peculiar skills the intimacies of marriage and parenthood require."

We are hearing today, more than ever before, about research in the behavioral sciences. James G. Miller defined them as "studies of the actions of men, their relations to each other and to nature."[12] Out of these studies will come new knowledge to aid women, and men too, in their own self-understanding and in their roles as parents and as husbands and wives, as well as knowledge that applies to many areas of life.

Many of the activities of the National Institute of Mental Health, for example, show a strong interest in studies bearing on child development and family relationships. A 1958 report included listings of studies on the improvement of communication between parents and teenagers, the effects of a mother's employment on the child's adjustment, and how the child perceives and understands influences to which he is exposed, as in the family.[13] One area of the Institute-supported research is devoted to marriage counseling. The entire list illustrates the shift taking place in our study of mental health. No longer do we look at the individual alone; we see him in relation to his family.

Even more research is continually adding to understanding in the field of human growth and development and its application to family relationships. It is these understandings and experience in seeing how they apply to real life problems that our college-educated future mothers and wives need in order to carry successfully their responsibilities.

These illustrations merely suggest what would be involved in organized study around a given area of home and family living that draws together knowledge from many fields and in so doing builds its own depth. College students need this kind of study organized around significant areas of home responsibility.

It is from the colleges that we expect to get our leaders in all walks of life. Dr. C. E. Rothwell, President of Mills College, according to a recent newspaper report, emphasizes the need for two primary goals for undergraduate education: (1) to give students "sufficient breadth to have some familiarity with the universe of knowledge at all its points, and therefore have a sense of direction"; and (2) "to give the undergraduate student the deep satisfaction of working in one subject in depth so that he becomes an expert." My contention is that today's world calls for a third kind of education—education in combining and applying, from the depth that specialists provide us with, the knowledge, understandings, attitudes, and abilities needed to carry on essential functions in our society—such as leadership in the family. This kind of education goes beyond giving the student a "sense of direction"; it gets her started in moving in that direction.

The college will have to make special provision to help women students to envision their future responsibilities as wives and mothers, and they will have to encourage joint efforts among faculty members in aiding the student to use the wealth of knowledge that is available and growing from related and interrelated disciplines. In such an institution the home economics department will be expected to share its wealth of experience and, in working with others on the staff, to extend and deepen those offerings designed to prepare students for creating a sound, healthy family life for all its members.

Competence for successful family living is needed now more than ever. The college today is challenged to place a high priority on preparing each student to carry her responsibility for leadership in the family and as a cultural force in the community, and her share of responsibility for the education of her sons and daughters.

DEVELOPING COMMUNITY LEADERS

ANNA L. ROSE HAWKES

The world has changed greatly since 1884 when Chester Arthur was President of the United States. Our nation numbered 33 states with a population of approximately 78 million people and an annual national income of 18 million dollars. Agricultural depression was reflected in the Agrarian Crusade and later in William Jennings Bryan's campaign for full silver. A sign of things to come had been the organization in 1881 of the American Federation of Labor under the leadership of Samuel Gompers. Another sign of things to come may well have been the organization in 1882 of the Association of Collegiate Alumnae. This preceded the organization of the W.A. of Collegiate Alumnae by two years, and the organization of the Southern Association of College Women by twenty years. Later these organizations merged to form the American Association of University Women.

Picture, if you can, a world with no telephones, no electric lights, no trolley cars, no automobiles, no buses, no radios or TVs, no airplanes, no mechanical housekeeping gadgets. Picture also a world in which women rarely worked outside the home, except as domestic help or as teachers, and a world in which very few girls went to college. The only organizations to which women belonged were missionary societies and sewing circles.

Girls had quite a struggle to obtain the privilege of going to college.

The Association of Collegiate Alumnae listed three questions to be answered by any thoughtful young person who sought a college education and who was willing to make the effort to attain this objective: "First, what especial value would a college degree be to her as an individual? Second, if there were values in each degree, how best could she assist in forwarding the aims and ambitions of other young women who also wished such training? Third, how best could she fit herself into her community and play the part in its life and progress which was at once her interest and her evident obligation?"

These questions are as pertinent today for candidates for college to answer as they were in 1884. I question, however, whether today one prospective candidate in ten considers the possible value of a degree to herself as an individual, or thinks of her responsibility in forwarding the "aims and ambitions of other young women" to this desired end, or questions how she can best fit herself in the life and program of her community, once graduated. I doubt whether it occurs to her that, because of the privilege of her college education, she has an obligation to the society of which she is a part.

This is not said in sharp criticism of our young college women today. The attitudes of her family and friends toward college and the colleges themselves are as much at fault as the girl. A good deal of the burning determination of those Victorian maidens to go to college was undoubtedly because so many institutions did not admit women and also because so many men of the middle and later 19th century proclaimed loudly that women were not fitted for college physically, emotionally or intellectually. That charge had to be disproved at all costs and disproved it has been. Today there is practically no institution of higher education that is not open to women, except the independent and denominational colleges for men. And long since it has become an accepted fact that women, too, have minds.

But somewhere along the way for women, the bright, sharp edge of going to college has been worn down. If the edge of going to college is worn down, then the college girl of today would of course be little interested in turning her energies to forward the aims and ambitions of other young women whose interests are as dulled as her own, and she would feel little responsibility for fitting herself into her community.

The attitude of parents toward a college education for their daughters has changed since the eighteen hundreds. In 1870 a certain John Todd, who is lost in obscurity except for his opinion on a college education for his daughter, wrote: "Alas! Must we crowd education upon our daughters, and, for the sake of having them 'intellectual' make them puny, nervous, and their whole earthly existence a struggle between life and death."

In the second quarter of the 20th century another father said to an interviewer who was urging an able young woman to apply for college admission: "A girl wastes her time in college and then just gets married anyway."

Professors, too, get this idea. Only recently a professor at Syracuse

University published an article in a national magazine with the title "Keep the Women Out of College." His thesis was that this was the solution for the anticipated over-crowding of our colleges. But when the staid *Wall Street Journal* takes up the cry with a front page article on "Feminine Fall-Out," it does not seem strange to see that many prospective candidates for college take pause. No one questions any longer the ability of girls for a college education. Only the validity of their objectives and the permanence of their motives are under fire.

However, this discussion is not the value of a college education for women. I am committed to discuss the position of the college woman as community leader. This includes women's training for their task, the public need for their service, and finally, their own conception of what their role should be.

Recently a college asked me to speak on the subject "Changing Patterns in Women's Lives in 1970." This is part of a series called "The World of 1970." I have not had much experience in prophecy, and I was reminded that when Saul wanted information about the future, he consulted the Witch of Endor; the Greeks consulted the Oracles at Delphi; the Romans consulted the birds. But I could only consult my own imagination.

A number of predictions have been made for the decade and the years ahead. One article in a New York newspaper based its predictions, not, it said, on a "free-wheeling imagination" but on "responsible reports by scientists, industrial leaders and technical editors." According to this oracle we shall wake up in "dreamland," in a house with collapsible panels, so that when we are tired of a square room we can make it triangular! Light bulbs will be a relic of the past; homes will be completely air conditioned, the same system cooling it in summer and heating it in winter; there will be complete soundproofing; buttons will let in the cat and let out the dog, turn on the light as we enter a room, heat conductors on the driveway to melt the snow, water the lawn, change the water in the swimming pool, wake us up with our choice in music, start the coffee, and warm up the car!

The article predicted a four-day working week, highways tinted rather than numbered, so that road maps will be obsolete. The telephone will be connected with TV, we will have meal-in-a-minute electronic cooking, disposable clothing, and automatic health-checking machines. The author did not state what need there would be for human beings, but my imagination tells me that women will be as necessary as ever, probably more so!

In the forseeable future, women will play a multiple role in our society. They will be homemakers and breadwinners, political participants and community workers. What kind of an education do women need for these tasks? Important as are the educational needs of women for the jobs of homemakers and breadwinners, the need for the education of women as citizens in a democracy is crucial. In a democracy we are obliged to provide better schools, better churches, better housing, better recreational facilities, and better programs of health and sanitation. In the American scene most of the responsibility for these programs which will help to build better communities is delegated to women. What kind of an education for these roles are young women getting in college today?

I believe the best training for those who accept their responsibilities as citizens seriously is a good basic liberal arts education. I think of liberal education not as an exclusive concentration on classical subjects, but as the *spirit* in which a subject is taught. Our young citizens should have an education that points up the relationship between the subjects studied in college and their function as members of society. A young political science major should not be content year after year transporting patients to the crippled children's clinic and develop no interest in possible legislation concerning handicapped children.

Education for community leadership should be one of the important goals of present day colleges. Consider the opportunity offered for this purpose. In our colleges today are all the future community leaders of our nation. Isn't it wasteful to let them graduate with little stimulation and motivation for their roles as such leaders and with little help in developing an attitude of thinking that is quick to see the relationship between cause and effect?

Some mental hospitals are said to use a "mop test" in determining whether or not a patient is ready to be dismissed. The patient is given a mop and taken to a basement where several faucets are running fast and overflowing the basins. If the patient mops and mops, without making any effort to turn off the faucets, he is taken back upstairs. Could not some such test be devised for college graduates to show the degree of their qualifications as citizens and community leaders? An English major should show some concern, for example, for better library facilities for every citizen; a sociology major should be interested in youth groups in the underprivileged section of her community; a music major might discover the great need for a young people's chorus. The possibilities are endless, and the college which does not provide this liberating function in the liberal education of the young women is not fulfilling its obligation to society. It is instead demanding of its students too much attention to mopping and too little to turning off the faucets.

In the second place, there will be a tremendous increase in the public's need for the leadership of women in every area of life in the coming years. By 1970 the work week is expected to be a four-day week of 30 to 35 hours. In addition, another ten or fifteen years will be added to the average life expectancy of people. Many thoughtful people believe that leisure will be the great problem in the decades ahead.

In the foreword to the volume on "Recreation in an Age of Automation," of the *Annals of the American Academy of Political and Social Science* (September, 1957), Paul Douglas has this to say: "Americans are experiencing a change in the structure of their lives in relationship to the content of time and the pace and values of living . . . It is characterized by new quantities of 'unsold time,' energies unspent in the economic process and disposable income above the requirements of the minimum necessities of living. As a result, enjoyments once reserved for a privileged elite are becoming widely distributed. The new concept of man in relation to time gives promise, in an age where tempo has been quickened by the application of atomic concepts and electronics, of the flowering of a great culture."

Not disputing Mr. Douglas, but warning us of the dangers of greatly increased leisure is Reinhold Wiebuhr. In commenting in an article in *Fortune* on the most important economic problem to be faced by the United States in the next twenty years he says, "Ironically enough, the productive power of our industry threatens to make our culture subordinate to our economy. *Too much leisure* may become a disvalue and lead to the disintegration of personality."

Neither of these gentlemen related their prophecies to the effect they would have on the lives of women, but even the most superficial consideration of their comments suggests many implications for the patterns of women's lives in the immediate years ahead and for the need the nation will have for her services in the community's cultural development. Women have always been the "culture bearers" of the race. The creative use of this new leisure will demand more of women tomorrow than it does today.

Fortunately women are endowed with active minds. They are discriminating and inventive, builders of culture, creators of institutions, and selectors of goals. In the face of the greatly expanded need for their leadership, women will not fail.

Finally, what do women themselves conceive their role to be? In a speech at the 1959 AAUW convention, Judge Mary Donlan commented thus: "Let us not be concerned for women's rights. Let us leave to the men any war there is of the sexes. What American women want is quite simply, I think, the opportunity for exercising, not for themselves but for the common weal, that citizenship right which is now lawfully theirs."

Women have come a long way since 1884. No longer are they hampered by long skirts and tight corsets; going to college does not concern the family for their health or their mental stability; their presence at the voting precinct or in political or educational conventions causes no stir in the audience. Women have come of age and, as Judge Dolan has said, they want only to exercise their citizenship rights.

I do not mean to imply that women do not want first of all marriage and children. But if they have even a little imagination, they know that they will have longer of their lives to live after their youngest child is in school than they had lived up to that point. And they know, too, having had the benefit of a good liberal education, that their role is not to sit and ponder the complexities of life, but to bestir themselves and try to relieve some of those complexities.

The political picture is changing also. In 1900 the feminist movement was devoted to denying any distinction between the sexes and to promoting the idea that men and women were equal citizens under the law. Fifty years later, although women had achieved citizenship, feminists were admitting differences between the sexes, but urging women to enter political life for the defense of interests which are considered to be their special concern.

Professor Maurice Duverger, professor of political science at the Universities of Paris and Bordeaux, is the author of the UNESCO study on *The Political Role of Women*. He reports that the political role of women is small and grows still smaller as the center of political leadership is reached. There are few women candidates at elections, fewer women members of parliaments and congresses, still fewer women as heads of government departments or in cabinet positions or as ministers. Where there are women in senior administrative posts, they tend to concentrate in specialized matters, such as health, education, family and maternal welfare, and problems generally considered to be of special interest to women. M. Duverger attributes this situation not only to masculine opposition, but also to the lack of vigorous resistance to this attitude on the part of women.

However, we must not be satisfied with the prohibitions which this modern world puts upon the full utilization of the intelligence and skills of women. We should recognize that they come from strong ideological blocks and from the traditional definitions of the nature of the differences between men and women. On the one hand, we can assure ourselves that the inequalities in women's opportunities which still persist will eventually be eliminated; on the other hand, we must face the fact that public opinion is slow to change. People cling to old ideas, even after they have ceased to correspond to the facts.

"The paradox of women," says Margaret Mead, "who are educated like men and can do most of the things men do, but are still taught to prefer marriage to any other way of life, causes most of the confusion that exists for women today." Women are brought up to be dependent on men! We are taught from babyhood to be passive, personal and maternal, docile, acquiescent and retiring. We are warned not to express our opinions too vehemently and not to contradict, even when we know the answer.

Masculine initiative and independence is encouraged and applauded on all sides, but these qualities are not thought to be feminine. This setting of the pattern of life into a man's world and a woman's world, has done harm to boys too. But it has had more effect on the personalities of women than of men, and when it perpetuates the idea that marriage and motherhood and full partnership in economic and civil life are completely irreconcilable, it becomes particularly dangerous.

Sometime back I listened to a radio program presented by Edward R. Murrow, called "The Educated Woman." I was greatly disappointed by the presentation, particularly in the comments made by college women as to what their college education had done for them. They were pretty vague about what college had done for them in the way of shaping their thinking, and not one of the women who spoke indicated that her college experience had given her any sense of responsibility whatever for service to her community, not any feeling of obligation to the society of which she is a part. That is pretty shocking. Never has there been such a desperate need for trained leadership as there is today, both volunteer and professional. Many women do contribute productively to society through volunteer work in the community. But countless communities need women for leadership in all sorts of necessary and productive activities: educational, social, political, and religious. Schools, hospitals, political organizations, and churches are all in need of a college woman's trained judgment, fresh ideas, and well-informed common sense in necessary and dignified services.

If it is true, as Ashley Montague says, that the intelligence of which the world stands most in need today is the intelligence with which women are most abundantly endowed, the kind of intelligence which ensures and conserves life and makes life more abundantly possible, then college women should be in the vanguard of those who are minded to question some of our social and economic issues and who are ready to tackle situations patently detrimental not only to home and family life, but also to national and international relations. Women have become today a social and an economic asset, an integral and essential part of the whole. The world cannot long survive without their contribution.

The world tomorrow will not be the world we have known. It will be a dangerous world, with the new demands of under-privileged nations for their inherent rights and with the threat of new weapons and with the continued and even increased competition with nations determined not only to equal our achievements but to surpass them. It will be an uncertain and insecure world, a divided and a competitive world, a small world, a restless world, and a changing world.

All of these characteristics of the world of these next decades will have their influence on women. Perhaps the characteristic of change will leave a greater impact on women's role than any other. The best prediction is that by 1975 the population of the United States will be approximately 226 million people. That means that for every three persons in the United States today, there will be 4 persons in 1975. What are the social needs related to this growth that may affect women? A great deal more housing and many, many more schools and teachers and equipment will be needed; and a greatly increased food supply and greatly expanded social services to meet the needs of these additional sixty-one million persons will be required.

In addition, the increased life expectancy and declining death rate mean an unusual increase in the number of dependents on the productive age group. And even if women do not have to provide the financial cost of these dependents, though that may be possible, they will certainly have the care of them.

The Labor Department predicts that there will be approximately three million more women than men in the United States in 1975, as compared with the actual one and one half million in 1958. This means, of course, that fewer women will be married ten to fifteen years hence than are married today. With the lower mortality rate and longer life expectancy, more women will be obliged to take care of themselves and their families, and they will have to bear a heavier burden of responsibility for public interests than in the recent past. Many more complex psychological adjustments will therefore have to be made by women.

Out of the wars and depression of the first half of this century, women have become identified in the total life of this nation. Their place in the world has been redefined. They have brought to the community and to the country what the centuries have taught them. In the widening relationships of these changing times, women recognize that they must bring their peculiar talents to bear on community problems. Their duties to their families are not diminished because other duties are demanded of them, duties with horizons as wide as the world.

Through thousands of years women have learned to recognize and to tolerate differences among individuals; they have developed a liking for and an understanding of people, a tolerance and a spontaneous ability to cooperate. They have developed organization and social order. They have also, out of the personal quality of their contact with people, achieved faith.

It is this organization and cooperation, this appreciation and understanding of people, this faith, that women bring to their role of community leaders.

In an unpublished epic written many years ago by a young woman for presentation by a woman's organization, are these lines, appropriate to my topic—

"The Times demand that women think;
Think not in patterns which were cut by other hands
And fitted to a world that is no more.

The Times demand that women act—
For women, now, can stand together and can choose
To build a better world."

When I was in Japan some years ago I heard this story from a Japanese woman about herself.

In 1955 the International Federation of University Women planned a conference in Manila of all the Asian Federations, of which Japan was one. The planners of the conference were a little disturbed about the complicated matter of the relations of the Japanese delegates to those from the other Asian countries. No Japanese had been in Manila since the occupation, and feeling there, even 10 years after the hostilities, was very tense. But they felt they could not humiliate the Japanese Federation by not inviting them; so they decided to let matters take their course.

Mrs. Yamazaki was at that time the Chairman of the Committee on International Relations and as such was the chairman of the Japanese delegation to the conference.

At the first session of the conference, the chairman of each delegation was asked to bring greetings from her federation. When Mrs. Yamazaki rose, she opened her remarks by saying, "We have come here to apologize for the outrageous deeds of our Japanese soldiers." Her speech received favorable publicity in the press, and people stopped the Japanese delegates on the street to compliment them and thank them for what they had said. But Mrs. Yamazaki knew there was still hostility, for she is a sensitive woman. At one tea given for the conference, she and the other two Japanese delegates met a group of Philippine Gold Star Mothers who were not slow to express their feelings. All the suffering and resentment of those years under Japanese rule came out, and the Japanese women took it all.

On the way home Mrs. Yamazaki said, "We must do something to prove to these Philippine women that the things they suffered at the hands of our soldiers are not approved of by the Japanese people. We must show them that we are a people who want the same things in life that they want; that we want to be friends, that we have discredited our military and that we regret what happened. Wouldn't it be wonderful if we could invite them to come to Japan and see for themselves?" The other women discouraged her—it would cost too much; you could never get people interested; and anyway the

Philippine women wouldn't come.   But Mrs. Yamazaki was not to be discouraged.

She got home the end of January, 1955.   She began talking to people, to organizations, to newspaper editors, to members of Parliament.   She even had an interview with one of the royal princesses. She started a movement which was finally supported by 27 organizations, every big city newspaper in Japan, and by the end of April that group had raised 3,000,000 yen, a sizeable amount of money in any language.   They invited the Philippine women, and they came, and the longest bridge of friendship in the world was built.

Who can estimate the contribution of this indomitable woman and thousands like her all over the world?   As community leaders, such women are invincible.   Their education, their sensitiveness to the problems of people, their ability to organize, their willingness to cooperate, and their faith in something greater than themselves make them think and stand together and choose to build a better world.

WHAT TO LOOK FOR IN A CAREER

ANNE ROE

A woman can get nothing from a career outside the home that she can't get in any other way, but some things may be easier to get in an outside career than in other ways. However, an outside career does not provide the most effective answers for certain other needs.

A career in this context means a sequence of related occupations pursued by anyone over a number of years. In some instances natures of the different jobs a person may hold throughout his life are very similar, the changes being chiefly in locality, seniority, income, and so on. In other instances marked differences may be seen between the job initially held and that in which one finally settles. If successive jobs are practically unrelated, it is hard to think of the sequence as comprising a career in any meaningful sense; there needs to be some thread of continuity and relatedness throughout most of the sequence for it to be a career. In this sense, of course, homemaking and child-rearing are true careers. It need not be true, however, that the end is foreseen, and that all that goes before is a planned series of steps to an anticipated climax; indeed, this sort of history is exceedingly rare. Even those who have some sort of goal in mind, if it is different from a beginning occupation, usually progress towards it in a series of steps which involve primarily seizing opportunities as they arise, rather than definitive planning.

Whether one works from choice or necessity—or elects to stay home—a career should somehow enhance one's life, should enrich it, should add more to the fullness of that life than it may take away from it. Work can detract from living; time spent in one way cannot be spent in another. A career, then, should be an integrated part of a whole life, not the whole of it, not something hitched onto it grudgingly. It may be a central part of life, a focus for most other aspects of living (as it is for most men). It may be quite peripheral but nevertheless an integrated part of a life, a part which fits harmoniously into the total structure. Well integrated or not, a career does affect all other aspects of living, and it is worthwhile to keep in mind how it can affect these other aspects when thinking about choosing a career. If a girl chooses a career as wife and mother, it is her husband's choice of career that will affect her life.

Perhaps the most pervasive of these effects has to do with the people associated with. Most working people make more acquaintances on the job than they do in other ways. If more than one person in a family is working, if they work at different things, and if all have even moderately social habits, the situation of each is less limited. However, in the usual life-time situation, and particularly in professions or occupations of long-term work with one firm or similar organization, people meet those who work with them. Of course, membership in a church or in a social club or an active hobby which leads to contact with others will widen social horizons. Too, some occupations are much more clannish than others.

Different occupational groups have different customs, and even different standards of conduct, although standards of conduct may be imposed by society rather than by the occupational group. A case in point is that of the schoolteacher. In many communities in this country, a woman teacher is still not expected to smoke, or to be seen in the company of other than a very select few, or even to marry, and many more restrictions may be placed on them than on most members of the community. Contrast this with the kinds of behavior not only tolerated but to some extent encouraged in such occupational groups as actors.

The kinds of communities one lives in may also be directly affected by the occupational choice. Some occupations—nursing or schoolteaching or office work—can be carried out in communities of almost any size. Others, such as merchandising, advertising or entertaining, are possible only in large cities.

Length of working day and the part of the day devoted to work both vary with the job. For most occupations the hours are usually in the 9-5 or 8-4 range, or day shift versus night shift. In any event, the hours are set and regulated and are not changed except under exceptional circumstances. There are other occupations, particularly among the independent practitioners, in which hours are extremely irregular and the working day very long—for example, journalists, reporters, physicians, and so on. The hours worked by school and college teachers are longer than they look to outsiders. A study of faculty members at a college of education showed a median of 58 hours and 25 minutes per week, with one fourth of the faculty working more than 66 hours a week. Yearly schedules may be affected in terms of seasonal fluctuations in the work itself and in the amount and timing of vacations.

Furthermore, marriage is affected. Both men and women marry within the same occupation more often than they marry outsiders, and this is also true for occupational levels generally.

Even such matters as health and longevity have some association with occupations, probably the result largely of the factors that condition choice of occupation rather than of aspects of the occupation itself. There are, however, some working conditions that are more likely to bring about certain health problems than others. An obvious example is the possibility of direct effects on the body from materials handled. There are also differences in the incidence of psychosomatic and mental illnesses which are associated with occupation, but these have not been very fully studied. Low income creates problems of nutrition and hygiene generally, but it also creates psychological problems, as does low prestige. It is not surprising that these can be reflected in the incidence of mental illness. On the other hand, one should select an occupation that will not increase major or even minor health problems.

An even more important consideration for most women is the effect upon their children of their working outside of the home. Many, if they can, deliberately refrain from this when their children are very small, believing with much justification, that it is better for small children to have their mothers with them. When the children are of school age, however, much of the logic of this argument is lost, particularly if the mother is not working full time. So long as the children are adequately cared for and continue to feel loved and cherished by their parents, no harm should come to them just from having a working mother. In fact, much good may accrue. There are, however, some special problems raised if one child's mother is working, but none of the mothers of his friends are.

There is an aspect to having a mother working that is too little considered. In their discussion of the American family, Parsons and Bales[1] have remarked: "A primary function and characteristic of the family is that it should be a social group in which in the earliest stages the child can 'invest' *all* of his emotional resources, to which he can become overwhelmingly 'committed' or on which he can become fully 'dependent.' But at the same time in the nature of the socialization process, this dependency must be temporary rather than permanent. Therefore, it is very important that the socializing agents should not themselves be *too* completely immersed in their family ties. It is a condition equally important with facilitating dependency that a family should, in due course, help in emancipating the child from his dependency on the family. *Hence the family must be a differentiated subsystem of a society, not itself a 'little society' or anything too closely approaching it.* More specifically this means that the adult members must have roles, other than their familial roles, which occupy strategically important places in their own personalities. In our own society the most important of these other roles, though by no means the only one, is the occupational role of the father."

Surely the occupational role of the mother may also play a very important part in this same way. Her wider contacts, her special knowledge, her colleagues or associates may significantly widen her child's horizons. The enrichment that her career gives to her own personality can also enrich her child.

What kinds of enrichment, then, can a career bring? I have said that a career is only a part of a life, and that it should be integrated into life so as to enrich it. But a much more fundamental question must be answered first. What is a rich life? What satisfactions, what experiences must we have to fulfill ourselves? Our highest moral duty is to be fully human, to know what we are, and to live it to the best of our ability. But to know what we are is not easy. And many persons do not know what they really want, or what they want most, or even what they must have to live a satisfying life.

Perhaps we should first consider what needs all humans have, and how these are affected by what they choose to do with their lives. Although all humans have needs in common, these needs are not of the same strength in all of us, nor is the pattern the same, so that something that matters very greatly to one person may not make any significant difference to another. We must find our own patterns.

In thinking about people and how they live generally, the approach of Abraham Maslow is as helpful as any.

Maslow thinks of people as having eight groups of needs which are basic, although some are more urgent than others. All of them are powerful in the sense that they govern our behavior, and frustration of them leads to deep dissatisfaction, to physical and emotional disturbances, and even to death. He thinks of these as being in an order of strengths, with the strongest, and as he calls them, "lowest," requiring satisfaction in order to maintain life, and the others appearing only when these are satisfied. He arranges them in an order from the most urgent and insistent to those that we can live without, physically speaking. Until the earlier ones are satisfied, the others do not appear, in the sense that they do not motivate our actions. His list from the most to the least urgent is as follows:

1. The physiological needs.
2. The safety needs.
3. The need for belongingness and love.
4. The need for importance, respect, self-esteem, independence.
5. The need for information.
6. The need for understanding, to understand.
7. The need for beauty.
8. The need for self-actualization.[2]

If an individual were dropped on a desert island, he would first be most urgently, in fact probably totally, concerned with only his needs for food and drink. Once these were satisfied the problems of shelter and protection from danger would become foremost, and then he would think of companionship and his other needs. Maslow believes that the most direct way to develop a life rich in satisfaction of the higher needs is through adequate gratification of lower needs— with adequate gratification they recede into the background, and attention can then be focussed on other things. It should be noted, too, that this order of strength is one he considers usual but not necessarily the same for all persons. (I myself consider the need for self-actualization stronger than those for information, understanding, and beauty.)

Maslow does not make a particular point of inborn differences in the strengths of the basic needs, but these surely exist, and the differences are of considerable importance for the development of different personality patterns, of different interests, and even of different career patterns. It also seems highly probable that there are quite consistent sex differences in the relative strengths of some of these needs, and these are relevant to the very real differences shown by the sexes even, indeed, from the day of birth. But let us examine each of these needs to see the role it plays in a whole life pattern and to see in what way a career can contribute to its satisfaction.

Physiological Needs. Such needs as for food, drink, and sex are

physiological. They are the most powerful of all needs. When
any of them cannot be gratified, one tends to become dominated by
them, and other needs just fade out of the picture. These are all
recurrent needs, and this dominance does not develop through tran-
sitory lack of gratification or even through moderately prolonged
lack when the means for gratification are known to be shortly available. What is important for physical—and mental—health is not
immediate gratification whenever the appetite appears, but the certainty of the possibility of gratification within a reasonable time.
Such a possibility is usual in our country now for most of these needs,
except for sex, and in general any threat to gratification of the others
is economically based.

It is clear that in our culture (except for farm families) the usual
means for satisfying most of these needs is available in return for
money, and for most of us, the source of money is a job—our own, a
father's, a husband's. So far as the achievement of these satisfactions
is concerned the source of the money is irrelevant.

The Safety Needs. More often gratified than not in our society,
at least for adults, are safety needs. We see them in action more clearly
in children, in their direct reaction to bodily illnesses, absence of
parents, to the appearance of strange, unmanageable stimuli, and in
their usual preference for an organized and moderately routinized
world. We seldom have to worry about unexpected bodily danger
except in terms of diseases or traffic accidents. The child's preference
for order and routine and the not uncommon preference among
adults for familiar rather than unfamiliar things as a steady diet,
are probably related to these needs. The known is safer than the
unknown, hence the quests for knowledge and for understanding
may have linkages with the safety needs, although they seem more
than subsidiaries.

Provision for these safety needs, like the physiological needs, is
primarily an economic problem in our society, and again the source
of the money is not of itself particularly relevant to the satisfaction
of the specific need. Money makes it possible to rent an apartment,
or buy a house, and to be provided with clothes, and with the sanitary
techniques and medical care that cut down the incidence and severity
of disease.

But in a long-range sense, the particular job held by the wage
earner may make a very real difference. Needs do not disappear
with the end of the working period, and provision for satisfaction of

them must be made, if not by the wage earner, then by society. One should consider how important this sort of long-range security is and how much of it will be dependent on the job. An individual may choose a job which promises security, in terms of job continuity, pensions and savings, over one which pays more and may even be more interesting but which does not give long-range security.

Needs For Belongingness and Love. People need and want a place in their own group and affectionate relations with other people; some need this more than others. The thwarting of these needs is, in our society, one of the most common causes for unhappiness, for neurosis, and even for more severe mental illness. We know that infants deprived of all affectionate handling may not live, that children growing up without normal affectionate relations will be retarded. These needs involve not only receiving but also giving love. Like all the others except the physiological needs, they can be lost without loss of life. In the psychopathic personality this loss appears to be permanent, and there is no known cure.

Probably the need for affectionate inter-personal relations is, on the average, stronger in women than in men. Most occupations can offer a great deal of satisfaction to the needs to be a member of a group, to have companions, to give and receive affection. To work with a congenial group, to be an intrinsic part of the functioning of the group, to be needed and welcomed by the group are important aspects of the satisfactory job. The extent of personal interchange on the job varies greatly, of course, not only with the type of job, but with the inclination of the persons involved. There are many job situations in which these satisfactions are more important than any others as there are some in which these are minimal.

Such satisfaction can be obtained elsewhere, sometimes more but often less abundantly. For women who follow a homemaking career these needs may be very adequately satisfied in informal neighborhood contacts, and particularly with the addition of club or church groups which seem to develop closer integration among their members. But a woman at home all day, alone for the most part or dependent upon her own small children for companionship, may well feel deeply unsatisfied. For many women who leave work for homemaking, the adjustment is a most difficult one, perhaps the more so because she may not realize just what she is missing so much.

Needs for love and belongingness apply in a special way to the parent-child relationship. For the very young child usually all of these needs are met by the parents. He cannot satisfy their needs in the same way, and yet there is a quality to parental affection and responsiveness which can rarely be experienced in other situations and which is truly an aspect of a rich life. An even more specific aspect to this (which I think very few men ever experience) is a kind of communication between a woman and an infant which is hard to describe because it is not intellectual or emotional and perhaps often not conscious; it seems to be almost on a physiological level. But it is communication, and it is genuinely two-way communication. It is not limited to a woman and her own child. I learned it on the job, many years ago, when I joined a group of research workers in a hospital who were studying new-born infants in such matters as the development of nursing behavior, variations in responsiveness, and so on. I spent most of my time in the hospital nursery or in the delivery room, or in the wards when the babies were taken in to be nursed. There is nothing else I know that is quite like this. It is approximated, perhaps more richly, but differently, by the sort of unspoken and often half-conscious intimacy of two people who have lived or worked together in affection for a long time.

The Esteem Needs. One needs to have the respect and esteem of others and to have respect and esteem for oneself. We need to feel competent, to be certain of our capacity to cope with whatever we may meet, and we need to be recognized by others as having this competence. There is some clinical evidence that the perception of oneself as competent and worthy of respect derives in part from the observation that others perceive one so. Thwarting these needs produces feelings of inferiority, or weakness, and of helplessness. If one is actually competent, or could be, but is so disparaged by significant persons around him that he cannot believe he is, he may indeed become incompetent.

Like satisfaction of the needs for belongingness, satisfaction of esteem needs can be a very important part of a career. Entering upon an occupation is seen in our culture, for a woman as for a man, as a symbol of adulthood and an indication that he or she has reached a state of some independence and freedom. Indeed, in our culture any adult male who does not have a job is suspect. This is not true of women, but there are very few places in this country now where a woman loses esteem if she elects to work.

In America it seems that the social and economic status of a man depends more upon his occupation than upon anything else. But the status of a married woman is more dependent upon her husband's occupation than upon her own. For the unmarried woman in a small town the more relevant factor is likely to be her family's position. Only in larger communities is she rated in terms of her own occupation.

The dissatisfaction felt by many women whose only function is the care of a small home, especially for those without children, is often related to the fact that there just is not enough in this occupation alone to give her a sufficient feeling of accomplishment to meet her esteem needs. Sometimes her needs are met by special personal accomplishment in such things as cooking, sewing, decorating, gardening, and the like, but these situations are becoming fewer. Her husband plays an important role in satisfying her esteem needs, but because he is receiving many of these satisfactions in his job and needs fewer of them from her, such satisfactions can seldom be adequately returned. In any case, esteem satisfactions depend upon the favorable judgment of one's equals, and very few husbands are equals when it comes to cooking, sewing, and so on.

Then, too, persons whose life situation is especially difficult may find that the status and prestige conferred by the occupation or received from fellow workers are the greatest sources of satisfaction for these needs, particularly in the case of members of minority groups who may receive an acceptance occupationally which they cannot achieve socially, or who may gain social acceptance through occupational status. The psychological burden of special disabilities may also be considerably relieved if a disabled person can hold his own with nondisabled on the job.

The Need for Information. Perhaps the need for information is better called curiosity, or a need to explore the world. We don't know what kinds of disturbance follow serious frustration of these needs, but this does not mean deprivation does not have serious consequences; it may only mean that they have not been recognized as such. We have not investigated this. But some people are actually afraid to learn, and this fear is truly a serious matter, probably resulting from frequent punishment or derogation for curiosity or inquisitiveness.

Anyone who has watched children grow up knows how the normal child accumulates and treasures items of information and seeks for understanding. They are constantly exploring, and questioning— so long as they are allowed to do so. "Why" is probably one of the most frequent and maddening (to the parents) words in the four-year-old's vocabulary. But how many children are so thwarted then that the need is buried? How much in our school practices is designed to encourage active questioning on the part of the child rather than passive acceptance of what he is told? A number of school problems are probably to be understood as the frustration of this and succeeding needs.

I suspect that this need may be one of those with consistent sex differences in strength, for whether the difference is culturally or biologically determined, it certainly seems to be a stronger motivating force in boys and men than in girls and women.

The strength of the need for knowledge and the quest for its satisfaction are clearly related to such things as the pursuit of a college education and the preference for an occupation which requires, or at least permits, continuous seeking for new knowledge. The particular sphere or spheres in which knowledge is most desired and the breadth of one's interests is also subject to enormous variation. Entrance into the learned professions is almost (perhaps not quite enough) limited to those who thirst after knowledge. Very strong motivation of this sort is required for those who go into research, along with considerable need for personal independence.

But even lesser degrees of this need for knowledge play a role in job satisfactions. Almost any kind of work is more satisfying if the worker knows what he is doing and why, and how it fits into the total picture. (Of course such knowledge may also enhance your feeling of belongingness.) The practice in the Army of "briefing" men for missions, the elaborate development of sales meetings, and so on, are recognitions of this fact. To do senseless work is pathogenic.

An appropriate occupation is certainly one of the best places to satisfy the knowledge need, probably the best place. However, knowledge can be pursued anywhere, and under any circumstances, but few of us engage in any organized pursuit of it on our own. We can have recourse to a library or to classes, if these are available where we live, but whether or not this search is satisfying depends upon the consistency with which it is pursued. Travel can be very satisfying in this way, if it is buttressed with some intelligent observation. The care of children, not to mention the care and feeding of husbands, can be very enlightening occupations. We can learn little or much in any situation, depending upon our openness to experience, and our willingness to reflect upon it.

The Need for Understanding. Related to the previous need, but not quite the same, is the need for understanding, which involves not just knowledge about aspects of the world but integration of this knowledge into a world view. To some people understanding seems very unimportant; to others it is an intense craving. We have never evaluated the results for the individual who is forbidden areas of inquiry and understanding because of political or religious ideologies; hence we do not know what kinds or degrees of disturbance may result.

Interpretation of the world in terms of some religious or philosophical scheme is a part of every known culture. For many persons it is enough to accept uncritically whatever variety of religion or philosophy is most familiar and to reject all others out of hand; for others it is necessary to work this out for themselves. Even those who accept some "authority" unquestioningly usually incorporate this unwittingly into a scheme of values, act upon it, and derive satisfaction from it.

Some occupations offer possibilities of satisfying these needs, but they include certain theological and philosophical occupations, and scientific research in its broadest construction, and women rarely pursue these areas.

The Need For Beauty. Maslow postulated the need for beauty on the basis of common experience rather than of clinical or laboratory research, and we have no clinical information on its frustration, again probably largely because we haven't looked at it. We do not know how closely the need for beauty may be related to particular sensory or other capacities which we do know to vary from individual to individual. Beauty is present in more than art or music or words; aesthetic emotion may arise from perception of patterns of ideas, of harmonies in living.

For those with great need for beauty, and appropriate capacities, various artistic vocations bring their own satisfactions. But these needs can be partially or considerably satisfied in other occupations and in many activities of persons who are neither trained nor particularly interested in formal artistic endeavors. A harmoniously decorated and orderly home, a well-planted garden, a nice piece of carpentry, these are all surely satisfiers of our human need for beauty.

The Need For Self-Actualization. All that one can be one must strive to be if one is to be happy. The more one is fitted to do, the more one ought to do. The specific form that this need will take varies with the capacities of the individual. Self-actualization may or may not be expressed creatively, at least in terms of products which are detachable from the individual, but all creative activity is an expression of it. It will probably always be expressed creatively in terms of life style. Effective self-actualization, however, can emerge freely only with prior satisfaction of the physiological, safety, love, and esteem needs, and perhaps some of the others. When it has emerged fully it seems to organize and to some extent to control these other needs, and may become prepotent over any. There are those who have preferred death to denial of their inmost selves.

This need seems less likely to have specific concomitants in terms of particular occupations, but (given appropriate work) its strength may well be the key factor in differentiating those who put enormous yet easy and pleasant effort into their work from those who do not. Happy effort and the amount of personal involvement in the work are probably the most important factors in success in any work, given the necessary basic capacities to do the work.

The self-actualization need appears in other than characteristically creative behavior. Walker and Guest, discussing the frustrations incident to a mass production job, suggest that the feeling of anonymity, of becoming depersonalized, is more disturbing than either the boredom or the tension that arises from repetitive and mechanically paced work. Certainly the more potentialities the job draws upon, the more satisfying it can be. The right job for the right person makes sense only in such terms as these.

Genuinely creative behavior can probably emerge only at the level of self-actualization. But such behavior may or may not have enduring importance. As much genuine creativity can go into the making of a home or the evocation of rich personal relationships as goes into the production of a great work of art or of a new scientific theory.

In summary, a career provides an income which makes possible the satisfaction of physiological and safety needs and aids in the satisfaction of other needs. But, the career of anyone within the family may provide these gratifications. Any career, in or out of the home, should provide opportunities for being with other people, both informally and in working with others to a common end. We should receive from any career the satisfactions that come from knowing that we are doing a good job and that others know it. We should have a sense of personal identity and a sense of community identity, of how we fit into the larger social group of which we are a part. If we are interested in constantly learning, we should look for this opportunity in a career, although we are unlikely to find broader philosophical understandings. For some, aesthetic satisfactions will be in considerable measure obtainable through a career, but for all who wish them these are available elsewhere. Finally, the career we choose should help us be more fully ourselves, to develop and use what capacities we have. For it is only by making the most of ourselves that we can make our greatest contribution to society.

THE MYTH OF THE MARRIAGE-CAREER CONFLICT

Marguerite W. Zapoleon

If life exists on other planets, perhaps somewhere on Mars at this moment some group is discussing the division of work on that planet between the feminine and the masculine of whatever species of thinking beings may exist there. This basic problem of how to divide between men and women the work that we need to have done is at the root of the so-called marriage-career conflict. In our world of today such a conflict is as unreal as a myth, but, when believed and acted upon, can generate trouble.

Even on this planet there are many ways in which different societies manage the division of their work, as our anthropologists have so vividly described. There is no one best way, suited to every time and to every place. But we are concerned with how it is handled today in the United States of America. Unlike the South Sea Islanders, unlike the men and women who fashioned our country out of the wilderness, we live in a society where public education, lengthening life spans, and technology have reduced the differences in what women can do occupationally as compared with men, and have lengthened the time women as a group have available for other work besides homemaking. The result of these influences appears in our statistics on women homemakers and on employed women. It is also evident all about us in our own families and circles of friends and acquaintances where we find more women working outside their homes but also more brides, more babies, and more comfortable and attractive homes.

The United States of today is very different from the United States of 75 years ago, a time when pioneering studies were just beginning to attempt to locate employment opportunities for college women outside of teaching; and when the Association of Collegiate Alumnae, the predecessor of the American Association of University Women, felt it necessary to undertake a research study of its members to disprove the then current notion that higher education actually affected the health of women adversely.

Although our statistics for that period are admittedly inadequate, there were probably about 1 out of 6 or 7 women employed then as compared with 1 out of 3 today. Most of the women at work outside their homes in those days were young and single. Opportunities for education and for marriage, like those for employment, were more limited for women then than they are today. Currently, too, we find that 2 out of 5 women working outside their homes today are 45 years of age or older, while in the 'eighties older women were exceptional in employment.

These few contrasts between now and then can only suggest the tremendous changes that have occurred in the past 75 years in the division of work in our economy between men and women as well as between man and machine and between home and work establishments. The production of what we need, once centered in the farm and the home, has been taking place in larger and larger units where specialization, expertness, and the use of expensive equipment and machinery have increased the quantity and generally improved the quality of goods and services. Men as well as women have been affected by these changes. In a sense the farmer who works exclusively all his life on his own farm may be compared to the woman who works exclusively in her home throughout life. We still need and have millions of farmers and homemakers of this sort, but not nearly as many of them in relation to men and women in other pursuits as we had in the last century.

From this viewpoint of the so-called dismal economist, the growing employment of women outside their homes is an inevitable result of our changing methods of production. It is further increased by changes in consumer demand which seek more and more of the type of services and goods that women are adept at supplying. In this view we see a widening of choice of occupation for women, and for men, too. The farmer who can now earn cash income in a nearby plant may be compared to the housewife who can earn money in an accessible hospital, store, or office. Where, then, is the conflict?

The very way in which our subject is phrased, *marriage-career* conflict, indicates that we are not thinking in simple work terms, or of work outside the home as distinct from work inside the home, but we are comparing two very different things. We start off with words charged with emotion and psychological connotations and are confronted with a semantic hurdle. The word *career* comes from the French word *carrière* meaning the course one runs, as in a race. It has come to mean the course one follows in life, and since occupation affects that course, it is often used to mean continuing progress in an occupation. Few people, today, however, follow the same occupation all their lives. And, if they do, they are likely to find the nature of the occupation itself changing with the times. A more realistic term for both men and women is *occupation* in the sense that Webster uses it, as our principal business or that which occupies most of our time and attention. Homemaking in this sense, and as used in vocational guidance, is an occupation along with those for which we are paid. Over a lifetime women and men, too, change their occupations, and some divide their time between two concurrent occupations successfully, although emphasizing one.

Marriage, the other term in our mythical conflict, means that a man and a woman choose to travel their life course together. Obviously a conflict between them will occur if they disagree about their destination, about the division of work between them, about the division of money, or about any other problem affecting their partnership. How each partner should spend his or her working time is a matter for mutual agreement. Like all other agreements it should represent a compromise between what they as a couple want and what they can have, as well as a compromise with each other in which each modifies what he wants for their common good. Where there is this kind of partnership, there will be no conflict about the work each one does any more than there will be conflict over the raising of children, over finances, or over any other major aspect of their life together. There will be many problems and many joint decisions to make regarding the work each pursues. But if a conflict occurs, it is not between the marriage and the occupation of one or the other, but between the man and the woman. And it stems from a failure to agree on common goals and the methods of working toward them. Any single area of their disagreement is merely a peg on which to hang their basic conflict. Unfortunately in the United States we seem especially prone to seek such pegs, to find a simple answer to a complex problem. And so, if a woman who works outside her home becomes separated from her husband, her neighbors are inclined to blame the break in their marriage on her employment. It is much more likely that the failure of her marriage has driven her into the labor market.

As we examine the so-called marriage and career conflict, then, we find we have something quite different to consider. Actually we have two different sets of possible conflicts. The one set relates to the possible conflict between the partners in a marriage, one that can be avoided through careful choice of partners in the first place and joint planning thereafter. The other relates to a possible conflict in allotting working time, particularly for women in allotting their time between homemaking and other occupations. The facts belie any general state of conflict among women on this subject. Women on the whole are aware of a more complicated set of problems and decisions that wider occupational choices have brought them and their families. But they appear well able to deal with these problems. Relatively few, clinging to the past or to fantasy, fail to accept our changing division and methods of work.

Nevertheless, the frequent mention of women's conflicts and dilemmas about their work roles, the implication that they are inevitable, may make ordinarily secure homemakers, working wives, and single career women, too, wonder if their feeling of satisfaction in their work is illusory. We all know that confidence can be undermined or reinforced by the expectations of others of our failure or success, especially in these days of "outer direction," as Social Scientist David Riesman has termed it, and especially in the case of young women who have not had the opportunity to disprove by experience the necessity of conflict between their work in their homes and outside.[1] Clinical Psychologist Marie Jahoda suggests that psychological problems have been created for women by the pressure for what she calls "the one right answer" with regard to patterns of living for women, each of whom must find a necessarily unique solution to her unique set of problems.[2] The Director of the Children's Bureau, too, has commented that the contradictory attitudes in the community are making working wives feel guilty because they work outside their homes. Another type of pressure on the homemaker, too, has been noted by Sociologist William Whyte. He claims the suburban homemaker is made to feel guilty if she is not carrying a backbreaking load of civic or social activities.[3]

A variety of writers representing many disciplines—psychology, psychiatry, anthropology, sociology, and the social sciences generally— have pictured homemakers variously as unhappy because their work lacks prestige, or is not a full-time occupation, or makes them overly dependent on their husbands, or makes them dull companions, or isolates them. The working wife is pictured as forever harassed and torn between her work at home and outside, too tired to be a good companion to her husband, a prestige threat to him because she earns money, or just as a flagrant violator of tradition. And single women working in our classrooms, offices, laboratories, libraries, hospitals, and factories are described as fearful that their work there will make them unsuitable for marriage or are made out to be compulsive workers finding an outlet for their frustrated homemaking needs. On reading the literature about women and their woes, a woman may begin to wonder if something is wrong with her if she is satisfied with her lot. That most women are actually satisfied with the particular roles they are playing in life has been proved time and time again in queries and polls.

All of us seem to have a basic need to be useful which we satisfy through our work, whether at home or outside. With the transfer of so much of our work to special workplaces and away from our homes, it is horrifying to read that at least one psychiatrist finds work outside the home a kind of activity that is naturally foreign to women. She has suggested that childbearing and homemaking responsibilities call for nurturing qualities while work outside the home calls for opposite or assertive qualities. If only she could listen to the complaints of employers who accuse homemakers they employ of trying to manage their workplaces because they are accustomed to managing their homes! If only she could see the millions of women who need nurturing qualities on their jobs! Actually, among women as among men, there is a wide range of personal characteristics, some inborn and some acquired, some apparently related to biological sex differences, some having no connection with them. Current research, still in its infancy, is throwing light on the personality requirements in different occupations. Meanwhile it appears quite probable that sex differences derived from the difference in their reproductive function explain in part the concentration of women in certain types of employment, in the professional and personal services, for instance, and in clerical work, which may be considered a form of office housekeeping. Within the larger occupational groups, too, women tend toward certain pursuits. In the professions, they congregate in teaching and nursing; in manufacturing, in the apparel and textile mill products and the foods industries. Even the increasing but still relatively small number of women in occupations filled almost entirely by men usually bring to the occupation a special quality derived from their feminine characteristics or experience.

As anthropologist Margaret Mead has said: Society benefits when the members of the minority sex in an occupation are encouraged to make their special contribution to it, provided they are attracted by their natural liking and qualifications for it rather than by a neurotic drive to compete with the opposite sex.[4] We all know that such a drive, based on the equally erroneous belief that a battle between the sexes is inevitable, is as unhealthy as an assumed conflict between women's work in and outside their homes.

So much for opinion, but what are the facts? We may, in reply, start off with a question. Can 12 million women be wrong? This is the approximate number of women who find it possible to live with their husbands and also work outside their homes at any one time. Their homes and their jobs would certainly be in imminent danger if they were experiencing any deep sense of conflict about combining homemaking with outside employment. And all of us would be in danger if these women suddenly deserted their posts in our hospitals, schools, telephone exchanges, laundries, offices, restaurants, and other work places. Even if the single, widowed, divorced, and separated women who remained in the labor force each tried to hold down two jobs instead of one, the exodus of wives would leave many unfilled posts.

Most women work outside their homes for the same reasons men do, primarily to earn a living for themselves or to contribute to a better living for their families. Today, as in previous generations, wives take the heavier share of duties performed in the home while husbands assume the chief burden of breadwinning. The husband's outside occupation usually takes precedence over the wife's where a choice becomes necessary. Because women bear children and are needed at home to care for and nurse them in infancy, it is a natural and efficient division of work to have them combine these duties with other tasks done in the home. But in a society which recognizes individual differences, there should be nothing sacrilegious about altering this division of work if a particular couple finds it desirable to do so. In times of illness, accident, or aging we often see partners reverse their usual roles successfully. And sometimes two generations combine their households so that the older members of the family may keep the home fires burning while the younger, more employable members, become breadwinners for their parents, too. The extent to which employed women support dependents is generally underestimated. Some years ago the Women's Bureau examined several hundred studies of women in all types of employment, including 30 conducted during the period between 1935 and 1950. They all showed that well over half of these employed women were in some degree responsible for dependents in addition to supporting themselves.

But what about women with young children? Is it true that women neglect their children in order to hold a job? Even if there is no conflict between marriage and career, is there a conflict between children and outside work?

Again, if we look at polls of women's preferences and at the available statistics, we find that most women give top priority to children. But, being realistic, they expect to work to enhance the homes into which their children will be born, and they are prepared to help now and then to supply their children's needs. It is interesting to note that the employment of mothers varies inversely with the income of their husbands, whereas the employment of married women who are childless does not vary with income. The expensiveness of children of school age is reflected in other figures which show that the proportion of mothers of school age children who are in the labor force is even higher than the proportion of childless wives who work. On the other hand, the home needs of children under six keep more of their mothers out of the labor market. In March, 1958, for instance, one out of five mothers with children under six years of age was in the labor force as compared with more than one out of three of all women. And if we look more closely we find that very, very few of these young mothers find it possible to work full time, the year around. For instance, in 1956, when 30 per cent of all women with children under six managed to be in the labor force at some time during the year, only six per cent worked the year around on full-time jobs. These statistics prove that most mothers are in the labor market because of their children's financial needs and not to escape their responsibilities toward their children.

But however good their intentions, what about the results? Is it true that juvenile delinquency has been increased by working mothers? Those of us who have for years combed research studies for some evidence for this statement can find absolutely no proof of a significant relationship between employed mothers and juvenile delinquency. In fact, authorities on the subject of criminal behavior have concluded that it cannot be attributed to any single factor and that each juvenile delinquent is unique. Actually, we find that the effect of a mother's employment on her children may be beneficial or harmful depending on a variety of factors. It is the weighing of these factors that each mother who contemplates working outside her home must concern herself with. Among them is the quality of care available to her children during her absence and her accessibility in emergencies. A 1958 survey sponsored by the Children's Bureau showed that 3 out of 5 of the pre-school children of mothers working full time were taken care of by relatives or the other parent. While many mothers who are now working would undoubtedly prefer to stay home if they could afford to, there are others whose employment is beneficial not only to their families but to society as a whole. Those who are inclined to feel sentimentally that every mother's place is forever in her home may well recall the words of political economist John Stuart Mill, who observed in 1851: "It is neither necessary nor just to make imperative on women that they shall be either mothers or nothing; or that, if they have been mothers once, they shall be nothing else during the whole remainder of their lives. Neither women nor men need any law to exclude them from an occupation, if they have undertaken another which is incompatible with it."

Now let us return, for a moment, to the 34 million women who are usually giving their full time to homemaking when the Census Bureau takes its sample count. Are these full-time homemakers, who comprise by far the largest occupational group among women, unhappy because they don't have an outside job? Our home economists tell us that these homemakers, if they live in a rural area, average 9 hours a day on their home tasks. If they live in an urban area, they average 8. They appear to be fully occupied.

The picture we see, then, is one of women at work in their homes, or outside, or in a combination of home and outside employment. The growing demand for women's services outside their homes has helped to offset the decreasing need for their services at home that some women experience when their children grow up and when they themselves become more expert in managing their home chores. But other women may find outlets for their energies in aiding their husbands in their work. Others, as they grow older, may not be physically able to carry more than a reduced load of work at home. Others may find their home load actually increased, rather than reduced, because of chronic illness in the family. Nor can we generalize about young wives. Each woman must work out her own work pattern, doing this jointly with her husband when she marries.

And she must alter her pattern from time to time, as changes in her circumstances warrant.

Is the picture different for college women? It is the same in the wide variation of work patterns, but different in the extent of employment revealed. Blessed with above average intelligence, fortified with the knowledge and skills her additional schooling has given her, the college graduate should be able to contribute more than the average woman, and statistics indicate she does. One out of two women college graduates is in the labor force as compared with 1 out of 3 of all women. In every age and marital status group we find the proportion of women college graduates at work outside their homes considerably higher than the proportion of all women so engaged. Only among mothers with children under 6 is the proportion nearly the same. The latest count by education taken in March, 1957, showed 19% of women college graduates with children under 6 in the workforce as compared with 17% of all mothers with children of pre-school age. The fact that most women college graduates engage in professional work, too, means that they can continue to work longer than they might in other types of work. Among women 65 years of age and over, 23% of the college graduates are in the workforce, twice the proportion of all women in this age group who are found there.

The statistics and opinions given so far should have exploded the marriage-career myth. But if it still appears plausible, I am willing to leave it to be destroyed by individual observations and experience. I am certain it is utterly safe and not at all contradictory for young women to continue to prepare themselves for the industries of this age and for marriage. In their decisions about work and about sharing their life roads with others, their education should help them choose wisely and plan realistically, to avoid conflict in marriage and in work, and to acquire that cultivated mind that Mary Wollstonecraft long ago said was necessary to render a woman contented. With such opportunity, surely some future alumnae will have valuable experience to share with the women on Mars.

THE DEMANDS OF MODERN SOCIETY

Harold Taylor

It may be worth noting that the subject of women has always greatly interested men—a variety of men ranging from husbands, lovers, and poets to the garment manufacturers, educators, psychiatrists, psychologists, and the editors of newspapers.

Men, I think, have shown more interest in women than women have shown in each other, although I was pleased to learn recently that living with women in women's colleges teaches you how to be tolerant and how to live in a woman's world. Knowing women's colleges as I do, I think that if you can learn to live with women in a college you can live with almost anybody.

I wish to discuss the contemporary society in which women find themselves and to suggest some ways in which women can affect certain trends in the future society.

A passage in *Dead Souls* by the pre-revolutionary Russian author Gogol gives an approximation of the education which women were receiving in pre-revolutionary Russia and which is sometimes suggested for contemporary American women:

"Madame Manilov had had a good education. And a good education, as we all know, is received in a boarding school; and in boarding schools, as we all know, three principal subjects lay the foundation of all human virtues: the French language, indispensable for the happiness of family life; the pianoforte, to furnish moments of agreeable relaxation to husbands; and finally domestic training, in particular, i.e., the knitting of purses and other surprises. It is true that there are all sorts of improvements and changes of method, especially in these latter days; everything depends on the good sense and capacity of the lady principals of these establishments. In some boarding schools, for instance, it is usual to put the pianoforte first, then French, and then domestic training. While in others, domestic training, that is, the knitting of surprises, takes the foremost place, then comes French, and only then the pianoforte. There are all sorts of variations."

This passage represents an attitude which a large part of the world has taken toward the education of women. I understand there are some parts of the South where this same attitude exists and where an effort is made by families to protect their daughters from the violence of serious ideas or from the harms which might come to them were they acquainted with the reality of contemporary society. Gogol's version of what a woman's education should be is extended in England and in France to some segments of the English and French population. At the moment there is a controversy raging in England about whether or not women should receive an education equivalent in intellectual terms to the education received by men.

In that argument, which we settled in most parts of this country more than 25 years ago, there were those who said that women should not be educated in the same terms as men because it would be bad for them to get ideas and to move out of the kitchen into the community. In the discussion now current in England, letters are appearing in the *Times* from angry fathers who feel that college education would be harmful to their daughters.

This struggle, which in the United States has now been won, is still going on in even the most enlightened countries of the world. In Japan, for example, only in recent times have girls been given the opportunity, through edict by General MacArthur, to go to high school. In former years most of them stopped at the fifth grade. Now girls can enter a program of free education for six years in the elementary school and three years in high school. The Japanese woman is expected to stay home, look after the home, not bother her head about political and social affairs; the men of Japan go home if and when they feel like it. The attitude of the Japanese men to the education of women is in a primitive stage in which they are still wondering whether or not equality is a good idea. At the moment, Japanese women are still in the grip of a social system which gives to women a status which is approximately that of American women 100 years ago.

The situation of the Indian woman is indicated by clippings from the matrimonial column of the *Times of India,* published in Delhi. I have two examples: "Wanted," says the first advertisement, "an educated graduate match of 28 or over, well established in business or service for handsome and accomplished graduate girl of modern views and independent means." (The term graduate girl means one who has graduated from college.) The prospective groom is to write to a box—1243 of the *Times*—to tell about himself, his business situation and his prospects. A second item reads, "A well-educated widower, well placed in import-export lines, income over 1600 rupees monthly, from respectable rich family having properties, desires marriage proposal from home-loving, good-natured, charming, educated bride. Apply Box 10378 the *Times of India*, Delhi."

I talked with a group of 18 women college students at Lady Irwin College in Delhi about the problems of the young Indian woman in the new Indian society. The situation of the modern Indian girl is one in which her opportunities for a free life in Indian society are limited both by social custom and the caste system, by the secondary place given to women and by the fact that 98 per cent of the marriages of Indian girls are still arranged by their families. In the educated classes it is now often possible for a girl to have an opportunity to meet the man she will marry two or three times before they are married. This is progress over the early days.

In answer to a direct question as to whether or not they accepted the system of the arranged marriage in the terms of which the older generation accepted it, the majority of the women students to whom I talked said they preferred that their parents make the choice of a husband for them. They said they had so little experience in meeting young men that they would not be sure of their own judgment.

Contrary to the Indian experience, the situation of the woman in Russia is one of complete equality with men. The Russian woman has much greater equality with men in terms of professional opportunity than even the American woman, and much greater equality in terms of education. Education starts at the age of six and moves straight through to 16 or 18 and is applied both by community pressure, by school pressure, and by a standard curriculum. Women enjoy equality with men in occupations ranging from street cleaner to lawyer, teacher, doctor, and professor in the university, where all the opportunities are open to them in equal terms.

I came to my interest in women in large groups rather late in life. I always felt that large groups of women of middle age wearing hats were the most formidable force in America. The only thing to do was to get out of the way of that force and never be there when they were there. I have since discovered that it is the energy and initiative and the brains, the social conscience and the moral sense of American women which has made it possible for them to achieve by their own efforts reforms which in many other countries have not yet been contemplated, and which in Japan were only accomplished because General MacArthur gave directives. The Japanese assured

me that had there not been an American occupation and had not
the Americans put reforms through by edict rather than by Japanese
voting, the situation of the Japanese woman would have remained
static over the next fifty years.

The Japanese women are awakening to their own responsibilities
and are taking initiative now that they have the vote and now that
they have a better place in their own society. But they remind us
that in America the strong-minded, intelligent women with a sense
of social purpose are the ones who have established a creative attitude
both in our social life and in the community life of the country. It is
largely due to the efforts of women that the rights of women have
been achieved, that women now have the vote and that their place
in American society, if not that of equality in the full psychological,
economic, and social sense, is at least close enough to show us the
way to achieve full equality.

The energy of the suffragette movement contrasts sharply with
American society today. We are now in a peculiarly negative and
conservative time in America. We are alternately rigid in our attitudes to other countries and flabby in our attitudes to ourselves.
In Indonesia, when Mr. Van Doren's exploits on television for pay
were discovered, an Indonesian said to me, "This is an example of
the decadence of the capitalistic system, the greediness of your
youth, the corruption of your intellectual and cultural life. Here
is a young man of good family who has had the best education
America can offer, yet who is a miserable cheat, and who stands
before his country condemned for his moral attitude and for his
failure to uphold the ideals of intellectual honesty."

I had no defense against arguments of this kind since I, too, was
astonished at Mr. Van Doren's conduct. The Indonesian went on
to say, "This is, of course, a function of the capitalistic system.
You people in America are interested only in material ends, and this
corruption has now entered your intellectual life. We don't want
American ideas of democracy and capitalism in Indonesia."

I believe it is symbolic of our present social situation that the
"beat" movement has grown up in the United States. In a complacent
and money-ridden society, it is no longer possible to be a rebel
in the older American terms, since no one seems to mind, and there
is very little to rebel against. The "beat" movement is a declaration
by a minority group of American youth that America is busy about
the wrong things. America wants to put longer fintails on the cars

and shorter bearings in the head. The rebels of the "beat" movement
find their enjoyment in rejecting everything which America stands
for. They want to stay outside America, to form a group of outsiders
who have their own mores, their own aimlessness, expressed through
extreme forms of behavior which make no sense by any standards
of the American community at large.

For America, it is a time of questionnaires, of pre-tested opinion,
a time when new suggestions are greeted with reasons why they
can not be carried out, a time of referring things to committees, of
asking ourselves worrying questions about what we should do rather
than stepping forward and doing what we think.

The disease of conservatism and caution has affected our colleges
and the reform of education. The problem of the women's colleges
is not, as some critics have said, that they try to become carbon
copies of men's colleges. It is that many of them have accepted
the external standards of competition and competitive success as a
substitute for deep personal satisfaction on the part of the student
in the work she is doing. That is to say, many educators and members
of the public are arguing that the colleges should stiffen the curriculum
in order to develop more technicians and to mobolize "manpower"
and "womanpower," and that we should exploit the untapped resources of womanpower in order to strengthen the defense effort
and the industrial establishment.

In the national discussion of education this argument is applied
equally to men's and women's education. It cuts more deeply in
the case of the women's colleges, since many women are themselves
somewhat confused about what they want from life. Some women
want careers and marriage; others want a full life in the community;
others want the kind of recognition which comes from business and
social success.

The modern woman has been put into a situation in which a great
deal more is expected of her, and consequently she has come to
expect a great deal more of herself than she can fulfill on all fronts
at once. Of course the modern educated woman is responsible for
a great many more areas in the life of her society than she was in
former years. She is the key to educational reform in the schools
by her direct relation to the school in her community. She is the
person most often responsible for the local political reforms in her
community. At the same time she is responsible for entertaining
her husband's business associates, for being charming to all, par-

ticularly to her husband, for coping with the children and the house-work in a home situation which is more complicated by the simple fact that the modern home is better off than it used to be, and that it is bigger and is more involved in various kinds of social relations than it ever was before.

Whether or not this degree of busy-ness creates greater satisfaction and fulfillment for the modern woman is another question. It is the same question which plagues the modern man in America, particularly the intelligent college graduate who has joined one of the large corporations as an executive, and who, in a sense, is considered to be the model of the contemporary American man. We need to ask the question whether his success in material terms, whether his busy-ness, his progress toward conventional goals of success does not create such a state of mind that the modern successful man no longer knows what his aim in life really is. The fact of being recognized as an important person in an important position in society does not guarantee a satisfying life.

The main problem in education which needs attention lies within the educational system itself. It consists in the tendency of students always to be working at the right things for the wrong reasons—to be working in the field of science, not to enjoy the excitement of scientific discovery, but to become a scientific technician; not to study literature, philosophy and psychology to enrich one's knowledge of human nature and human life but to obtain high academic grades, to be recognized by a Phi Beta Kappa award and by a long paragraph in the college year book. These are artificial values. They are at present being presented as the purpose of education itself, when the true purpose of education is to develop one's inner self and one's capacities to serve the needs of other people.

At this point in the history of American society, young men and women are being diverted from these aims into a struggle to achieve false standards set by their society. The society is reflected in the education, rather than the education leading society to new levels of endeavor in the moral, spiritual and social dimensions.

The fate of women in this society is inextricably tangled with the fate of men. The very notion of equality of the sexes insures that the psychological and social security of women is bound up with the solutions which men and women find together for the problems of the modern world.

What are some of these problems?

As a country, we have been on the defensive over these past ten years. Immediately following the war, we found ourselves in a welter of new problems, many of which seemed insoluble. Our principal difficulty was that of accepting our position as the leader of the post-war world, the strongest country in the world, faced by an intransigeant and aggressive Soviet Union. In this situation we were led to adopt a policy of balance of power in military alliances to combat Communism rather than to develop a Wilsonian program of moral and political leadership.

At the moment we are losing more than the space race to the Russians. We have lost the position of moral and political leadership which should rightfully be ours, and we have done so by insisting that to be counted as our friends, other countries must join us in a political and military alliance against the Soviet Union and her satellites. The countries of Asia now suspect our motives in providing foreign aid, and there is caused resentment against the American attitude toward the newly developing political systems in Asia as a whole. The Asians find our foreign policy full of ambiguities. We support reactionary governments because they are against Communism, no matter what they are for. The Asians feel that they are responsible only to themselves for their policies in relation to Communism, and they do not wish to be told by the Americans *or* the Russians how to conduct their foreign policy.

As far as American policy is concerned, the way to surpass the Russians is not to become more like them or to make of our educational system an instrument of cold war policy. It is to return to the native American tradition of progressive social reform, of progressive ideas in politics, and to show by example, at home and abroad, what democracy means in action, and how democracy can work to solve the problems of world society.

If we are to reform our educational systems and develop new ideas for the education of women, we must face the fact that our educational system is not like that of the Soviet Union and that we can never be successful if we try to imitate the Soviet system. If we are to raise academic standards, we must do so because we wish to raise the standards of American intellectual and cultural life, because we wish to achieve greater success in the development of individuals who understand the modern world and who have high moral and personal ideals. We will not achieve these reforms simply by emphasizing heavy academic disciplines and more academic subjects.

We must involve our students in the work of the college community at a higher level of intellectual and personal interest than they now possess. We must make certain that when students study science, they do so as part of their general search for more knowledge and more truth, not merely to fulfill an academic requirement. When they study the arts and the social sciences, we must plunge them into the middle of their own time in order that they may understand new truths, so that they can then apply these truths to the lives they will be leading after college. We want our students to be participants in their society, not merely observers, critics, and technical experts.

We must therefore teach them how to deal with the race question, not only because it is a fundamental problem in American society, but because it is a moral question which must be solved if America is to assume her rightful position as the leader of the world. We need to deal with the race problem, not merely to attract the approval of world opinion, but in order that we can look upon ourselves with pride and dignity. By helping the Negro to achieve equality in the United States, we are doing ourselves the greatest honor—we give ourselves the privilege of association with the Negro; we gain from him a new kind of companionship in a democratic society.

We must also set to work to change the sense of aimlessness which affects a large part of our educational system, particularly in the larger universities where there is too little relationship between the students and the teachers. One example is the experience which the people of India have had recently with their university system. Three universities were closed last December because of student riots. These riots reflected an uneasiness in Indian society and were in part a product of the tradition of agitation against the government which students have inherited from the past struggle against the British. But fundamentally, the riots occurred because of the lack of central purpose in the lives of the university students. I found on questioning the students that their main problem lay in the fact that there was no leadership from the faculty to guide them and to give them a sense of the role they could play in developing a new Indian society.

The Indian examples are extreme in their demonstration of what can happen when there is no sense of purpose among students, no recognized place for the young in their own society. In America our problem is not as extreme, but the problem itself is of the same character as the Asian. The student must learn to know what his purpose is in attending the university and what his obligations are to his society.

In the past the women's colleges have shown leadership in the solution of this problem, partly because they have not been affected by the same social pressures which have plagued the co-educational colleges and the colleges for men. They have been freer to devote themselves to the development of each student as an individual, without the constant demands made in other institutions for vocational training and job-getting.

In the Soviet Union the students do have a sense of purpose and a sense of pride in their accomplishment as students. They are proud that the Soviet Union has built an educational system which provides them with a free education in contrast to the society before the revolution which provided no education for their fathers and mothers. Now all children have their own schools and are proud of being included in the student body. The students who go to universities feel that they have an honor in representing their country.

This sense of purpose, rather than anything which we may have heard about the qualities of the Soviet curriculum, is the source of the strength of the Soviet educational system and accounts for its unusual success in the field of science. Soviet instruction is no better than ours; the total program of the Soviet universities compares unfavorably with that of American institutions. But the concentration by the students in achieving the goals set before them makes a significant difference between the American and the Soviet results.

In the United States many students take for granted the privilege of receiving a higher education and, in the case of women in some of our larger co-educational institutions, the suggestion is often made that they are there to find a husband, to enjoy the social life. They carry out the academic duties of the college student merely to remain in a social community inhabited by attractive young men.

There is certainly nothing wrong in enjoying personal and social relationships in college, but this is not the reason for being in college. The central question in the relationship between education and our place in world society is, what kind of instruction must we have in order to give to our students a true educational aim and a sense of commitment to the ideals of their country?

One emphasis given to the reform of college instruction has been the use of television as a means of instruction. All of us in the field of education are happy to accept television as a useful instrument, just as we are happy to support the idea that documentary films are a legitimate and important means of instruction. But in terms of the central question, the answer is not to be found by increasing the number of lectures given over television or shifting American university and high school systems to the use of mass media for communication of educational values.

The emphasis on a mechanical solution, the emphasis on a larger amount of academic subject matter, the emphasis on higher grades to be achieved by everyone have diverted us from a more serious consideration of the individual human being whom we are attempting to educate. A statement by a student from a college for women identified the direction in which our educational reforms must move:

"The two things that a college can give that allow for true growth are time and aloneness. In an age when the jet plane travels so fast that the passenger has no chance to absorb the world he is passing through, the ability or the incentive to think for oneself is losing its needed time for growth. When there is time to think and with it an aloneness, as painful as the solitude may sometimes be, there is true opportunity for reflection. There is a saying by Tagore, 'Man goes into the noisy crowd to drown the clamour of his own silence.' Perhaps this can be paraphrased, Man accepts the belief of others to hide the emptiness of his own conviction.

"When in education the possibility of a teacher-student relationship is forgotten in the discussion of superior teaching over television, will there still be room for the illumination that comes when someone has said something directly to you that suddenly fits together something you have learned, opening the door that brings you a step forward so that you knowingly say to yourself, 'There I was, but here I am now.'"

By an insistent pressure, the atmosphere in college must be created to look within, not just without. This is the central insight around which the reforms of contemporary education should move.

In women's colleges there is more opportunity for reflection and for the development of a rich inner life. The modern educated woman has become the strongest force for liberalism and for political and social initiative that exists in contemporary American society. If we look at the American community, we find that the educated woman is at work there at a level where the most effect can be produced and where reforms function to move society ahead. I have mentioned the way in which modern woman has responsibility in her community for the kind of education which is practiced there. For example, it would be impossible to close the schools of the South over the integration question if the women in the Southern communities refused to have them closed. It is impossible to have bad teaching continue in the suburbs of Chicago or in the schools of New York if enough educated women in the communities are in touch with the situation and refuse to allow these conditions to remain. Because women are the strongest force for social change in the American community, the education of women must take as one of its central purposes the development on the part of the student of social sensitivity and a sense of obligation toward American society.

It is also true that the cultural life of the United States depends for its development, in large part, on the initiative and support given by women to the arts. The arts flourish where there is an audience for the arts, when there are sympathetic and keen critics, when there are those who have learned to practice the arts and to love them. No artist can function without those who love and understand what he is doing. If we are to have artists, we have to have educated young men and women who are themselves practitioners of the arts.

In the community where I live, in the suburbs of New York, the women are the ones who work hardest at the development of the cultural life—theater for children, the support of community forums, the organization of concerts of music and dance.

I would therefore say that, within the colleges for women and within the co-educational colleges where women are educated, the creative arts must be introduced as regular elements in the curriculum on equal status with those subjects so prized by Admiral Rickover and his supporters. The subjects of chemistry, physics, biology, and mathematics are fascinating, interesting, and important. But of equal importance, and in some particular ways of more importance, is the work of students in music, dance, theater, painting, sculpture. We require the invention of new forms of these arts and work in the arts by students who practice them, not in their spare time, not as if they were frills at the edges of the school curriculum, but as integral parts of the life of young men and women in America.

The responsibility of educating our children in the arts often falls into the hands of the mother of the family, since the father is away all day and out of touch with the opportunities to deal directly with his children as they go to school and learn the arts themselves.

Women who have not experienced the deep aesthetic satisfaction which is available in the arts are unlikely to communicate the importance of that satisfaction to their children. It is for this reason, among many others, that the education of women should include a full program of work in the creative arts. I do not mean by this that women should be given the traditional music appreciation course in which one reads about music and analyzes compositions. I mean playing the piano, singing, dancing, acting, writing for the sheer joy of it. This is the only way to understand and to appreciate the arts themselves.

One matter I have already mentioned; that is the matter of the heavy emphasis on lectures, examinations, academic grades, and related methods of instruction. Many of the high schools have suffered paralysis of the curriculum by the necessity imposed on them to provide a program which will enable students to get into college. Too much of learning has to do with discovering a series of points which can be written down in a notebook and delivered on schedule for the examination. When books are read to make a series of points, very seldom do they yield intellectual or aesthetic satisfaction. The lecture system, and along with it the examination and grading system, must be radically modified if we are to rescue education from its present weaknesses and to build upon its present strengths. We must return to the individual student and think seriously about the approach the educator can make to him and to her in order to build an education around the human needs and the educational aims which each student has. Martha Graham, whose expression as a dancer and a creative artist among choreographers marks her as one of our most original Americans, has this to say about the individual: "There is a vitality, a life force, an energy, a quickening, which is translated through you into action. And because there is only one of you in all time this expression is unique and if you block it, it will never exist through any other medium and the world will not have it."

It is our responsibility to take account of what Martha Graham has said. There is, in fact, only one of each of us. This expression of vitality and force is unique. If it is blocked, it will never exist in any other medium and the world will never have it. As the young girl grows up to be an educated woman, it is of crucial importance that she push to the extreme her talents and find the one identity which constitutes the person she really is. It is necessary not to accept other people's images of oneself.

When we take the development of individuals as a central aim in the education of women and men, we concentrate then on trying to help our students to achieve a sense of reality about themselves and a sense of purpose in terms of what they can do with their lives. Our students need to know the ways in which they can enrich their own talents and the ways in which they can use these talents for the benefit of their fellow men. Until they have learned to do this, they have not yet begun to live. To teach our students to live in these terms is the purpose of education.

DIVIDENDS ON HUMAN INVESTMENT

LEO C. MULLER AND OUIDA GEAN MULLER

The advancement and support of higher education is the concern of a great number of people, and it is receiving more and more attention across America. But it is the advancement and support of higher education for women, especially in women's colleges, which is particularly germane to this book.

While the case for women's colleges is excellent, their voices, for the most part, have been very faint, and they have not enjoyed the financial support their efforts deserve. Those which have are the exception.

Parallel with the premise that women must be educated goes the premise that someone must *invest* in this education. Parents are not able to bear the burden alone. Other sources of revenue must be discovered to provide opportunities for America's women.

The young women of America and the women's colleges in general should be able—logically and deservedly—to receive more of the monies presented to higher education. We are convinced that when the complete story is told, and told properly, women's colleges may be destined to enjoy a greater share of the funds which are certain to be invested in higher education in the immediate future.

To this end all must work harder in the decade ahead in the areas of institutional planning and effective constituent relations.

American women's colleges, and all colleges for that matter, must challenge corporations, foundations, philanthropic groups, and individuals to make a worthy investment in the higher education of women.

These constituencies have distinguished themselves by their support of higher education. But the problem now is how to direct a more proportionate share to the education of women. For, after all, "the democratic ideal proposes that the student, regardless of sex, should be allowed to develop to the fullest. Surely the right of young women to develop themselves academically, socially, culturally, morally, and physically should not be denied. In fact, paths should be found and lamps should be lighted by which they might be able to find the best route to realizing their destinies."[1] Many coeducational institutions of higher learning—the great universities like Indiana, to mention one—do a splendid job in the education of women, but this discussion focusses on women's colleges.

Whether a college be one of the better known private schools of New England, or a publicly supported college of the South, a private two-year college of the Mid-West, or whether it be the highly reputable Mills on the West Coast, if it is a women's college it usually has an excellent reputation and almost always needs support to continue to do the job it is doing.

Among the 258 women's colleges in America are the Catholic colleges extending from coast to coast, which do not enjoy support from the Catholic church, but which are doing a tremendous service to the nation in developing spiritual and moral values of young women. Private, public, or church related, the women's colleges in America are important in the higher education picture and are worthy of investment.

This importance is emphasized in excerpts from a report from the Council for Financial Aid to Education: "Colleges for women . . . excel in what they do. . . . Now that the United States is assuming international leadership . . . women . . . will undoubtedly have to become leaders in activities more complex. . . . The largest claim . . . is the contribution of alumnae in conserving humane and spiritual values in family and community life. . . . A woman's education is the education of a whole family."[2]

With these introductory remarks, let us now briefly consider: (1) the fact that women's colleges are not enjoying their share of voluntary support; (2) challenges facing women's colleges; (3) where the colleges for women need strength; (4) how the alumnae might help in the cause; (5) the role of business and industry and the colleges for women, and (6) a pattern for giving.

Women's colleges are not enjoying their equitable share of available financial support, and the lack of support is detrimental and growing increasingly so.

Speaking at the American Association of Colleges convention in 1960, Mrs. Opal D. David, of the American Council on Education, emphasized that changes in women's education have not kept pace with the changing times. She pointed out that women now have a longer life span, marry earlier, have their babies earlier, and many of them are destined to spend 25 years in gainful employment. Because of these factors she reasoned that women's educational patterns are lagging because the women's colleges are not getting the support they need from foundations and philanthropic organizations.

She declared, "It's a paradox, that a country where women control more and more of the nation's wealth is giving less and less of it to educate those women."[3]

Giving the background of why five college presidents resigned (four of them from outstanding women's colleges), Anne W. Langman alludes to the financing of higher education: "It is particularly arduous in women's colleges, where alumnae are not likely to have large independent means. A husband's big gift goes to his own alma mater; his wife's college is secondary." She remarked, however, that "A coed college like Oberlin has fund-raising problems too."[4]

That alumnae do not give proportionally to what their husbands provide for their alma maters was brought out in a study by a very respectable liberal arts college for women which prefers to go unnamed. The study tells of a survey of gifts to alma maters by husbands as compared with gifts by wives to their alma maters. Predictably, the women's colleges were on the short end—by an unhealthy margin.

The Council for Financial Aid to Higher Education, Inc. reported in a survey of giving in 1958-59 that corporate support for higher education was the fourth highest source of voluntary support reported by colleges.

A 1956-57 report showed that the 129 women's colleges included, which was 14% of the institutions surveyed, received a total of less than 5% of the amount distributed by the corporations.

This figure is even more discouraging when some comparisons are made. While the 129 women's colleges received less than 5%, 65 major universities received 43%, 109 state universities and colleges, received 12% and 66 private men's colleges received 4% of the total. An earlier survey (1954-55) by the CFAE also revealed that women's colleges received only a meager share distributed by business firms.[5]

In speaking of industrial support for women's colleges, President Otto F. Kraushaar of Goucher pointed out that "women's colleges received a larger percentage of their total support (including corporate support) by way of state or regional fund-raising associations than any other type of college." This, he felt, was further proof that "the appeal of the women's colleges is relatively weaker than other types."[6]

Convinced that business and industry were not giving a proportionate share of their financial support to America's women's colleges, the Dumore Foundation of Racine, Wisconsin; St. Mary's College, Notre Dame, Indiana; and the John Price Jones Company, Inc., of New York, a leading firm in the field of institutional fund-raising and public relations, made a cooperative study.

The survey showed that, except for the junior and municipal colleges and universities, "private women's colleges were . . . passed over by corporations in favor of almost every other type of institution of higher learning," and presented evidence that "in general, women's colleges enjoyed the attention and support of corporations to the extent of only 50 per cent or less of that enjoyed by other institutions of various types," which . . . "is a serious area of financial weakness for all of the 258 women's colleges in the United States."

The question of "why" corporations neglect these institutions which generally enjoy a splendid reputation for academic excellence may be answered in the survey conclusions, recorded here in brief:

1. Corporation executives "are not thoroughly familiar with the purposes, achievements and needs of women's colleges."

2. A rationalization of the neglect of women's colleges by corporations seems apparent.

3. An "emotional male prejudice against higher education for women", whether caused "consciously or unconsciously" is evidenced by corporation leaders.

4. "Women are employed in a greater variety of positions in greater numbers than is generally realized."

5. A majority tendency exists to deny any direct significance of college educated women to business and industry as employees, yet the study pointed out that " . . . there is already some basis in many cases for arguing the cause of women's colleges on the grounds of direct usefulness."

6. A majority tendency exists to recognize the "indirect importance of college-trained women" as wives, the purchasing power of women, and women as an "element of strength in our general social structure and community leadership." It was reported that "most firms can apparently be induced to give a sympathetic hearing to women's colleges on one or another of these grounds."

7. Excluding the possibility of a joint approach through a state foundation, more than one fourth (29 per cent) of those corporations

responding have not even been approached by women's colleges for aid.

8. The pattern of giving to individual colleges, to associations, to local colleges or colleges where corporate branches are located, or only for scholarships or specific purposes, was indicated as a possible reason for not giving to women's colleges.

9. *"Women's colleges are not yet doing an adequate job of selling themselves. They are not yet presenting the facts clearly enough, widely enough or forcefully enough"* (italics ours).

This excellent study also presented some recommendations: (a) "Women's colleges must arm themselves with facts, . . . to meet the demands of corporate self-interest and dissipate the miasmas of prejudice." (b) "Comprehensive statistics should be obtained concerning the role of college-educated women as a group, and especially the whole body of graduates of women's colleges." The survey recommended that "women's colleges . . . work together as a group to obtain and pool the necessary facts. . . ."

(c) "The active assistance of national educational associations and groups should be enlisted. . . ." (d) "Women's colleges should be prepared with full studies and statements on their financial needs when they approach corporations." (e) "In preparing the case for support by corporations, women's colleges should bear in mind both the indirect and the direct services which they render to industry and business." (f) "Alumnae employed by corporations should be identified and especially urged to contribute generously to their alma mater." (g) "Corporations should be urged to establish scholarships for daughters as well as sons of employees." (h) "Emphasis should be laid on the indispensable role of women's colleges as part of the total system of higher education in this country." (i) "Business men and corporation executives must be reached more directly and more often if their attitude towards women's colleges is to be seriously influenced."

(j) "A public relations program of increased scope and effectiveness is strongly indicated."

The last recommendation is particularly pertinent, for the survey elaborated, "Brochures and leaflets, newsletters, personal interviews, special corporation events, should all be developed to carry to the corporation executives in a convincing and insistent manner the facts about women's education and its significance to our society, and the financial facts about women's colleges."[7]

We hear a great deal about women having more wealth in their own right than men and about their also controlling even more of the family's income. Yet it has often been suggested that men are inclined to give more toward higher education, and indeed philanthropy in general, than are women.

It would be wonderful if, within the next decade, enough women, who actually *do* have the means and who actually *do* control the purse strings, proved this assumption to be completely invalid. It would be an even greater wish that women who are in a position to assist might not only equal the generosity of male philanthropists but even exceed it. Surely, women's colleges and colleges in general somehow ought to reach these women and convince them of the great need for an investment in continued educated womanpower.

Sometimes women are not in a position to give, but they can urge their husbands and their husband's friends to give. That this can be done with success was brought out in *Time* magazine (May 2, 1960) in a story titled, "Affectionately. . . . "

"For four generations, the Rockefellers have admired Wellesley College for women. No exception is Mary Todhunter Clark Rockefeller, wife of New York's Governor. Though not a Wellesley alumna (she graduated from Virginia's Foxcroft School, attended the Sorbonne for a year), Mrs. Rockefeller is a loyal and energetic Wellesley trustee. Two months ago, she fired off a letter to her husband's office, reporting that Wellesley's campaign to raise $15 million for faculty salaries was almost three years old and less than one-third to the goal. Last week she proudly revealed the tardy but profitable reply:

> 'Dear Tod:
> Thank you for your letter of March ninth concerning the Wellesley fund-raising drive. I would be delighted to contribute towards this campaign, and accordingly, this note is a pledge of securities having the market value of approximately $150,000, this amount to be paid at my convenience prior to January, 1962.
>
> Affectionately,
> Nelson'

"The biggest single pledge in Wellesley's campaign so far, Nelson's husbandly gesture swelled the take to $5,082,851. Even at that, Nelson was less generous to Wellesley than his grandfather, John

D. Elected as honorary member of the class of 1901, John D. was so pleased with being a Wellesley 'girl' himself that he shelled out $1,000,000."[8]

Women's colleges actually face peculiar problems, and women students themselves are often hindered by circumstances which place them at somewhat of a disadvantage.

Women's colleges do not get an equitable share of corporate giving; their alumnae are not "emotionally" motivated to giving to their alma mater, and the cost of educating women is more than that of educating men.

Chancellor Gordon W. Blackwell of the Woman's College of the University of North Carolina pointed out in *Women's College News* that "Plant operation and maintenances costs are higher in college facilities for women. Social areas must be furnished for students and their guests from neighboring colleges; programs in home economics, art, music, and physical education require specialized facilities; adequate security must be provided;" and students are usually required to live in the dormitories, another added expense.

Dr. Blackwell said, "A study of per capita appropriations for publicly-supported colleges for women in Georgia, Oklahoma, and South Carolina reveals that they all require more support than do the state universities or the land grant college."[9] This is as true for private colleges as for their sister public institutions.

Dr. Quigg Newton, President of the University of Colorado, listed some obstacles in educating women when he appeared at Loretto Heights College in the spring of 1960 to evaluate women and their role in college.[10]

First declaring that he felt girls are more conscientious and serious minded about their work "in many instances, at any rate," President Newton listed three impediments to their getting a good education: (1) often boys in the family get priority on funds available; (2) girls find fewer jobs available on the campus, and (3) girls find it harder to concentrate on their work because "they have a desire to please the boys to a point where it interferes with their education." Women's colleges help to solve the last problem, but these first two are all too true.

The male members of the family have heretofore without question received the nod for further education in the event it was a case of one sex or the other going to school. With the growing awareness of the desirability of women being educated, there may be a shift in parental thinking about the education of their daughters. Actually, more parents (although they may approve of higher education, even for their daughters) need to be convinced that their daughters can benefit from attending college as well as their sons, and that a college education should not be a privilege for men alone.

Some parents, fortunately, do not need to be reminded that girls have equal educational rights. But when a young girl does find her way to college, she finds it harder to remain there than does her brother or next door male neighbor. Men have more opportunities to secure scholarships, and they enjoy a wider range of part-time work opportunities. It would seem then, that money sent from home should be shared equally with daughters, and if a financial showdown occurs, perhaps the girls may need the heavier purse.

Of course, if part-time work or a scholarship cannot be obtained, a talented girl might get a loan through the National Defense Loan Act, which does not show prejudice because of sex. However, one writer raised a pertinent question when speaking about just how much a girl student will have to pay for her education. "Are loans to students going to be a major source of funds for higher education in the years ahead?" he asked, and then reasoned, "If this is so, what effects will this have on higher education for women? Will mortgaged brides be alluring?"[11]

Running throughout the pages of this book is a current of thought that explains the most significant reason why women's colleges need more financial support. This thought—and it is actually a reality—is that the needs of women are changing, and that these changing needs must be met by a revised, a strengthened, and a broadened curriculum—and it takes money to do this. Unless the women's colleges have adequate financial help, they can't begin to make the changes which are dictated by the urgencies of our present society. Elmira College, under President J. Ralph Murray, is one of the colleges altering its format in keeping with current and future needs. But other colleges must follow Elmira's example, and they cannot succeed without funds.

Even if women's colleges do have a sound case, if they are doing a highly acceptable job, if their needs are somewhat different from other institutions, and if they must change their educational patterns to serve the women of the future, it must be candidly stated that their lack of support has not been entirely the fault of apathetic constituents.

The truth is that the women's colleges have not told their stories convincingly or to enough people.

The situation is clear. If our colleges are to progress and to develop to meet the needs of those desiring a higher education in the future, if institutions of higher learning are to enjoy the great untapped resources of business and industry and other givers which are rapidly coming to invest in education, and if colleges are to expect the utmost from the alumnae in terms of financial support, a highly organized, diversified, and all-inclusive program of institutional planning and interpretation is both an urgent and an essential need.

American colleges, private and public, coed and exclusively for women, are destined to do an even greater service in the future; therefore, they *must* develop. This is why, throughout the nation, college and university presidents are striving to find clues to winning greater support from the people—through the legislatures, business and industrial grants, corporations and foundations, philanthropic endeavors, alumni, and every other potential source of revenue.

Faced with the tremendous challenge of providing higher education for all those who seek it, which necessarily means more expenditures for faculty and staff, buildings, scholarships, and other services, college presidents are rapidly setting up development councils for their institutions to organize and tell their stories in such a way that the listeners might be persuaded to invest in education.

Another cooperative way of calling attention to the needs of higher education is through independent associations or foundations. But even the smaller institutions must use their own initiative to tell their story and to seek assistance because the regional or state associations are supplementary, not primary, sources of voluntary support. Many colleges (among them a number of women's colleges) *are* doing a splendid job of presenting their case to various constituents and they are getting results. The future seems brighter.

But colleges must win the alumnae if they would win others to their cause, particularly private colleges which cannot look to public funds but must seek assistance from alumnae and other sources.

Generous gifts from alumnae are the keys to effective giving by business and industry. Business, industry and foundations are coming to the aid of colleges when they see the college alumnae believing in and investing in their own alma maters. Unless generous alumnae support is in evidence, corporate leaders wonder if the particular college rates the prestige it claims to enjoy.

Alumnae must rally to the support of their alma maters, but the colleges cannot ask alumnae to invest more simply by telling them what is true—that they did not pay the whole cost of their education while in school. Colleges must continue to provide services to merit their support.

In his address "A Plea for the Uncommon Woman," Richard Glenn Gettell, president of Mount Holyoke College, highlighted the importance of keeping alive "the adult interests of the young wife, during the years when she is all but submerged with home responsibilities, and [remembering] that at some future time she may wish to enter upon or resume a life beyond her immediate family interests."

This leading educator suggested:

" . . . women's colleges might do well to press further their efforts at designing refresher material for their graduates . . . to prepare and distribute periodic bibliographies of current reading in their former students' fields of concentration, or to call their attention to recent general cultural advances.

"Perhaps more can be done with the intellectual fare presented at alumnae meetings, and in alumnae publications. Perhaps more intensive summer institutes or other up-to-date courses could be offered alumnae. And these, I submit, should not be elementary or dilettante-ish as are some ventures in adult education, but should be at a high level, suitable for the intellectual quality of the best graduates."[12]

Chancellor Harvie Branscomb of Vanderbilt University said that "the generous giving of business, industry and big corporations and increased alumni support of higher education is the major educational development in our decade."

Business and industry, he declared, are helping support higher education, but "business has a right to ask of education, to *demand* of education, educated students and special services." He said that institutions must make certain that their houses are in order, that they are "an effective business enterprise," and that they maintain "the attitude of *noblesse oblige* in terms of responsible citizenship."[13]

But what about women's colleges? Are they actively seeking the support of business and industry? Some of them are, with a refreshing vigor. William R. Cole III stated in the *Commonwealth*: "Hollins— and other private colleges—look a great deal today to the businessman, and they want the businessman to look toward them. The establishment of true rapport between the college and businessman rests in considerable part on the recognition by each of the problems of the other."[14]

Carter Davidson, president of the all-male Union College, gave the education of women and the women's colleges a boost by this "conversation:"

"But," the corporation officer may interrupt, "many of your liberal arts students are women; some of your colleges are for women only. We employ practically no women college graduates, and then only in secretarial posts. What possible stake have we in college education for women?"

"I agree, sir, that your corporation may employ very few college women, though there are hundreds of thousands of them in corporation posts. Your firm, however, does market its product to consumers, the majority of whom are women, and your continued success may depend upon the educated perception of values among your women customers. Also, women hold or inherit half the property and wealth of America, including perhaps a large block of the stock certificates of this corporation; an intelligent, well-educated group of stockholders can be a wonderful asset for enlightened management. I should not neglect to remind you, also, that wives exercise enormous influence over their husbands, whether those husbands are corporation executives or engineers or research scientists or stockholders or merely buyers and sellers of your product—and wives who have been well educated in a liberal arts college should be able to contribute in no small measure to the corporation's success."[15]

And corporations can do the job. Speaking at the Indiana University Institutional Planning and Development Workshop in the summer of 1959, Dr. Frank A. Sparks, president of the Council for Financial Aid to Education, declared: "At present corporate earnings could easily take over the total needs of higher education—fifty billion annual earnings before taxes compared to two billion gift needs of higher education."[16]

If the women's colleges are as adept at wooing business and industry as women in general are at wooing men, we can envision a happier educational prospect for women. The colleges for women and the institutions wanting to serve their female students better need to develop the best type of leadership to help them develop to the fullest to realize their goals. Women's colleges need to excite the enthusiasm of men and women of the caliber of Frank Abrams, Irving S. Olds, Alfred P. Sloan and Frank H. Sparks. They need to

convince them—on a business-like basis—of the value of higher education of women, and especially of the part women's colleges might
play in leading the way in women's education.

Citing a study of the Public Relations Society of America on
corporate contribution practices, Rembrandt C. Hiller, Jr., director
of Civic Affairs for Sears, Roebuck and Co., noted: "The study
indicates an increasing recognition among companies that the choice
is not *whether* to contribute, but rather *how* to contribute. More
and more companies are developing new management techniques
for proper handling of contribution requests and contribution
dollars."[17]

Of course, giving must be voluntary, and givers will continue to
have the right to distribute their funds as they wish. In building a
case for a given institution, it would seem, however, that a positive
approach, emphasizing the good things being done or being planned
if resources are made available, might be a better approach than a
sneering or derogatory attitude toward a rival college. We need
less bickering and selfishness and more unity, not in terms of philosophy,
but in terms of a common respect and understanding for what the
other colleges might be trying to do and for their right to do it.

Too often large institutions and well-known or "prestige" colleges
receive the bulk of appropriations, grants, and gifts, while smaller
colleges must be content with a mere trickle of funds. It is time
that corporations, associations, and colleges and universities themselves understand that diversity of purpose among institutions is
necessary and good, and that the less famous college has as much
right to expand and develop as the "prestige" institutions.

Too many colleges are suffering from financial malnutrition. Francis
C. Pray, vice-president—college relations for the Council for Financial
Aid to Education, Inc., said that his travel about the nation gave
him "a new concept of one of the educational phenomena we are
now recognizing—the truly frightening speed with which the gap
between the high quality and the mediocre institutions is increasing."[18]

This gap may never be completely closed, but it must be appreciably
narrowed. No one would wish to deprive the large and well-known
institutions of the monies they need; they are entitled to substantial
financial support. But so are the smaller colleges. As long as the
philosophy of the school is conceived in the light of the needs of
students and society, as long as an institution strives to meet objectives
in tune with its basic philosophy, as long as there are students who

want its particular type of education and educators and citizens who believe in it, then that institution has a right to financial support.

More and more colleges are thinking today not only in terms of present needs but in terms of long-range planning, trying to pave a path for those generations yet to come. If these colleges are going to succeed in the future, the key will lie in cooperation between those who are willing to serve and those who are willing to invest.

The money is available; the corporations and others are willing to give it. They need only to be convinced to try to allot their funds more democratically to all those institutions which are trying to fulfill their purposes and which need the means to do so.

11

THE PROSPECT FOR TOMORROW

Leo C. Muller and Ouida Gean Muller

The American woman—what will she be like during the next forty years, at the dawn of a new century? One thing is certain. She will be at least partly the product of the educational patterns being created for her today.

The nation's colleges possess a high record of achievement in the education of women. They have educated thousands upon thousands, and they have been a guiding force of leadership in the continued education of women. Their collegiate and cultural heritages, the tempo of modern times, and the outlook for the future make their potentialities and challenges ever more purposeful. While not exclusively their mission—nor should it be—the colleges for women, by their very nature, might be destined to deliver an even greater impact upon this singular aspect of education.

From some of the best minds in American higher education, whose thinking is reflected in the preceding chapters, an attempt has been made to synthesize current feelings, facts, and trends in the education of women. In many of the areas there are divergent points of view, but this is to be both expected and encouraged; for only through healthy disagreement and continuous discussion of all opinions and philosophies, can education—or any other field, for that matter—continue to progress.

Purposes of the Higher Education of Women. Women have been attending colleges in America for over a hundred years, and out of this progressive century only one conclusion has emerged as generally accepted: women should be educated. But how they should be, and for how long, and for what are still philosophical swamps through which no firm road has yet been established. Part of the morass is the result of conflicting opinions on the role of the college itself, whether its function is to educate the mind or to educate the individual. And one of the most urgent problems facing American higher education today is the search for a set of basic educational principles in keeping with our present society and its needs.

114

Of the purposes conceived and suggested today, these seem to be most often mentioned: intellectual expansion and discipline, individual awareness, social consciousness, vocational training, transmission of the cultural heritage, creative expression and/or appreciation, and competency in family responsibilities.

That academic interests should be the primary function of colleges is not disputed, but when the academic disciplines are presented as the *sole* function of the college, then the dispute errupts. Many educators believe that the student should be able to relate the subjects studied to her role as a member of society, that the liberal arts must be taught in a liberal spirit. There is sharp disagreement as to how far the college should go in attempting to educate the "whole personality," yet most educators agree that in addition to intellectual needs, there is a wide range of basic needs and competencies which the college must either meet or help the student to meet. One of these is the drive for self-realization; another is for identity as a part of a group and as an individual, both of which contribute to the societal need for newer and better leadership.

In the area of education for women particularly, the battle lines are often sharply drawn. Women, it is conceded, are fully capable of attaining an education equal to that of men, but "equal" does not necessarily mean "same." It is argued that both the inherent role of woman in society and her changing role in society dictate a "different" type of education, one that will develop her intellectual powers, give her professional training, and provide her with the basic skills necessary to be a successful wife and mother. Indeed, this area of professional training is a critical one. Granted, a liberal education is the best type for women, some educators say, but professional training gives women a sense of perspective in their academic pursuits, as well as a sense of security and of creativity in later life.

When an educational philosophy encompassing these objectives and giving proper emphasis to each is developed, then the higher education of women, and indeed of both men and women, will have taken a giant step forward, equal, perhaps, to the progress made in the past hundred years.

Intellectual, Spiritual, and Moral Values. This mechanized age places great confidence in technical knowledge and skills, but the fantastic pace at which science and the world are expanding only points up more clearly the urgent need for understanding and wisdom. If ever there was an age when philosophers and intellectuals were needed, this is it. We have the technical skill to solve scientific problems, but we lack—or, at least, lack in abundance—the intellectual skill or human sensitivity to solve the problems of the world and of our own society.

The potential source of the thinkers needed in today's world is the college or university. Only from the well of the academic disciplines can we draw forth the intellectual, spiritual, and moral values our culture demands. To counteract the forces of materialism and Godlessness presently extant, there must be a revitalization of the spiritual and moral forces. It is not enough to know how to act when a rule applies; we must also learn how to act when there is no rule to apply, when the standards and ethics of conduct must arise from our own thinking and decisions.

But the bookworm and the academic hermit are not the solution; their main contributions have been in terms of history, not of society. Instead, there must be a renewed emphasis on the thinking, intellectual individual—and such a role is not an easy one. The intellectual must be willing to go against cultural pressures and community dictums; she must be willing to build a house without a picture window and a patio. She must guard against her personal isolation from problems and unpleasant conditions. She must reject complacency, foolish optimism, defensiveness, and self-interest, and accept curiosity, critical thinking, mental aggression, and a concern for the good of the world and future generations. Her personal life must be creative and expansive, guided always by perceptive clarity, tolerance, and individual independence.

The development of thinking individuals by the institutions of higher education and the encouragement of respect for the moral, spiritual, and intellectual values is our only road to national and global salvation.

The Education of Homemakers. Even though more and more women are working outside the home, and even though husbands are adding more domestic duties to their role, the primary responsibility for home management remains with the wife. Modern appliances, new products, and easier-to-keep houses and furniture have lightened the physical work-load considerably in the span of a single generation. But the mere possession of such equipment and facilities does not ensure an efficiently managed household; the homemaker must be competent enough to manage her facilities and to organize her time to the best interests of herself and of her family. Even the less perceptive homemakers become aware of their inadequacies and become frustrated with their home duties, often without realizing that the cause of their frustration may be simply a lack of training in basic homemaking skills.

But if home management requires skills, there are other, more important home responsibilities that require not only skills, but wisdom and understanding. Women are still the transmitters of our culture, of the moral, ethical and spiritual values that must be imparted to each generation. Accordingly, the homemaker must be aware of her role as a mother with all its implications. She must understand that she must nourish, not only a child's body, but his mind and personality, and she cannot carry out this task competently without understanding at least a few of the basic principles of child development.

The increasing equality of the husband-wife relationship, and all the changes in the traditional family structure that this implies, calls for new abilities and attitudes. As women's status changes, their relationship with their husbands and families changes also, and they should be prepared to cope with this change, to anticipate problems, and to work out satisfactory life patterns intelligently.

The knowledges and skills necessary to be a good homemaker can be attained to some extent without a college education; certainly it has been done in the past. But we are not living under past conditions, with past responsibilities, in past environments. Young women today need the knowledges and skills of today; they need to be taught to draw from a variety of disciplines those concepts and principles which apply to their present role. Many institutions are meeting this need of educated homemakers for an increasingly educated society. Courses in home economics are being set up to acquaint non-majors with techniques that they will certainly need when they become homemakers—and the majority of women will. In addition, courses in other areas and fields are often being presented in the light of their relationship to concrete problems and situations that occur both within and without the radius of the family.

Courses in home economics might be enriched by areas of study in communications, the social sciences, psychology, science, religion, philosophy, and others. Students and educators who have frowned too long on home economics might find within the content of many of the courses the precise prescription needed by young women to supplement their understanding in this basic area of homemaking.

It would seem, then, that in the broad sense of the term, instead of being only departmental, homemaking could actually be extended to embrace a large number of academic disciplines, that each student could draw from divergent areas of study those principles, concepts, techniques and perspectives that will help her create a sound, healthy family life that can contribute to the betterment of the world.

Women in the World of Work. The woman who spent her early years flitting from drawing room to parlor with a lace fan in her fingers and who in later maturity devoted her time to needlepoint and knitting—that woman cannot find her image in our society today. The completely dependent wife has little place in our culture. We expect a woman today to be productive, to contribute something to her family, to her community, to her society. In many cases, this expectation is satisfied by employment outside the home, either part- or full-time.

One-third of the women in America are working, and only one woman in ten can expect to go through life without ever being employed. Part of this is the result of streamlined production methods and jobs which require less brawn, part is the result of a larger core of trained womanpower than we have had previously, part is the result of alleviated home duties that give women more time to work outside the home, and part is the result (or perhaps the cause) of a new-found sense of independence in women.

But the causes are not as important as the effects. Originally, concern was expressed over the effects of working mothers on their children, but the children were found to thrive and grow as long as they had parental love. And there has been no correlation found between juvenile delinquency and the children of working mothers. Significantly, few mothers of pre-school children work unless there is a definite financial need for their employment.

The main effect seems to be one concerning the husband and wife relationship. The problem appears to be one of mutual adjustment to a projected pattern of individual and joint desires. It is when a compromise cannot be reached that a conflict between marriage and career occurs. The basic problem would seem to be, not one of marriage vs. career, but one of individual vs. individual.

As for the working woman herself, she is achieving new heights in self-fulfillment, particularly when she is able to participate in a field which enriches her life, which broadens her experience, which enables her to use her training and talents in a manner which she feels is contributing something to society, as well as to her family.

Today the trend is to educate women also along professional lines so that they may be assured of economic independence, of adding to the work force needed by the nation, of profitable utilization of their vacant time, of maintaining and developing their personal skills and abilities, of acquiring a sense of personal and community identity with a larger social group, and of liberating the individual.

Social Responsibilities of the Educated Woman. It took centuries of struggle for women to become recognized as citizens, and through those years they learned not only militance, courage, organization, and perseverence, but patience and tolerance, understanding and cooperation, and above all, faith. These are the qualities that suit women for the exercise of leadership. Add the catalytic agent of a good education to the fore-mentioned qualities, and the potential of women today becomes even more formidable.

Women are good at getting things done. They tackle a city slum with the same vigor and enthusiasm that they expend on a mud-spattered floor. They have decided more elections, built more schools, controlled more corporations than our still male-oriented society gives credit for.

But now that society has discovered the leadership powers of women, it must point out that they simply aren't doing enough. Despite their effectiveness, the number of women "doing" is still far less than the number "watching."

Women seem to possess in abundance the traits of initiative and leadership. But they must be encouraged to utilize these characteristics in the community, in the nation, and in the world. We need more Madame Pandits and Mrs. Luces, more Madam Chiangs and Mrs. Roosevelts, whether we agree with what they do and say or not. But we also need the Mrs. Smiths and Mrs. Browns and Mrs. Joneses who will probably go unrecognized on the larger scale, but who can be just as effective for good within their personal perimeters.

But even the woman who remains somewhat detached from civic and political affairs, who does not exercise as much leadership as her neighbor, still has a social responsibility. She must be prepared to instill in her children, among other virtues, a social awareness, a belief that evil can be overcome and that good can be accomplished—if only somebody will take the initiative. A woman who exercises her education in instilling leadership in others can be a leader, too. Indeed, the leadership qualities and the social responsibilities inherent within her may be expressed in even more far-reaching ways than she had dreamed possible—through her children. If being a leader is sometimes difficult, the training of tomorrow's leaders can be even more challenging; but for the unselfish person with faith in the future, it can be even more rewarding.

The Changing Role of Women. Our attitudes toward women and our conception of their role are undergoing revolutionary changes. Some of these changes are reflected in our way of life, which itself is radically different from what it was fifty, thirty, even twenty years ago. Young people reared under one existing group of conditions suddenly find themselves in an adult world where the conditions are quite different.

One of the erstwhile prevalent conditions was the notion that women belong in the home. Today's young woman sometimes feels guilty if she is content to remain by the hearth. At the same time, the working woman feels an occasional twinge of conscience that she is not devoting all her time to starching doilies, baking brownies, and bathing squirming little bodies. This feeling of ambivalence is a natural characteristic of woman's changing role. She is like a butterfly newly emerged from a restrictive cocoon, testing her wings and sometimes tottering feebly before she gains her full strength and soars independently.

The prohibitions and limitations put upon women's intelligence in the past are recognized as senseless and unfair, but while they are so recognized, women find they still exist in those areas not already allotted to women's special interests. Undaunted, perhaps even inspired by the blocks, women continue to seek new avenues for expression and performance—and they are finding them.

Women are destined to play an even greater part in society as the years advance. An expanding population and increasing longevity are resulting in more women, more older women, and more unmarried women. They will have to carry a larger share of responsibility for the public welfare, and at the same time, they must learn to handle their own psychological problems which will be arising with the change.

A great deal is expected of women today—far more than was expected of their mothers: they must be good wives, good mothers, good leaders and professionally trained, well-educated, and fully cognizant of their responsibilities as citizens. In turn, women are asking for greater freedom from societal and cultural pressures, greater opportunity for individual self-fulfillment, and a greater sense of independence. There can be little doubt that they will achieve all their goals, for what American women have achieved in half a century, through their own efforts, is amazing when their social conditions are compared with that of women in other civilized parts of the world.

But despite the advances, American women still need help in understanding the complexity of the role assigned them, help in formulating philosophies that will encompass new life situations, help in meeting the very real and concrete problems that will arise, problems for which there is as yet no one solution—all this, so that as even newer patterns of living evolve, women will be able to deal with them.

The Future Education of Women. In discussions about trends in higher education four general points usually emerge: (1) the need to inculcate a sense of purpose in students; (2) the need to encourage intellectual behavior; (3) the need to revise and strengthen academic offerings and techniques; (4) the need to change the prescribed educational patterns to accommodate different types of students.

Young women especially need to be imbued with the knowledge that their education is *for* something, that it is not going to be engulfed in the trivialities of a hum-drum world, that the knowledge they gain is going to be useful.

Closely allied to this need is the necessity of encouraging a respect for intellectual behavior. This involves primarily helping the student to do critical thinking, to approach problems and situations from a logical, intelligent point of view, uncluttered by prejudices and fallacies. The crucial problems developing within our culture and affecting individuals call for sober, deliberative thinking, not rash and hasty judgments. The student who is to put her talents and skills to the best possible uses must preface every action with sound, intellectual behavior.

It is generally agreed that the liberal arts form an excellent base for the education of most young people, but it is also agreed that the liberal subjects must be taught in the light of contemporary problems and situations, not in the dust of outdated traditions. The subject matter must relate society to the student and the student to her place within that society. Too, the techniques and tools of instruction and evaluation will need to be modified if the student is to gain the most from her education experiences and if the college is to assess properly her assimilation of knowledge. Some educators foresee a modification of the lecture system and a change in the grading and examination system. This concern is reflected in all areas of education.

Perhaps one of the most interesting predictions is that the colleges will find it necessary to alter their traditional patterns of education, particularly in the light of the needs of women students. There is a feeling that the bachelor's degree need not, indeed, should not, mark the terminal point in education. The reasoning is that a four-year block of time in late adolescence or early adulthood cannot provide for all the exigencies of life. It is an admirable base, and the best foundation to date, but the pressure on young women to marry early and to have families early often means that they fail to complete those four years. It is the thinking of some that young women who fail to graduate should be permitted to earn the remaining necessary hours at some later time at some other college, and that certain residence requirements be dropped to enable them to do so. There is also some interesting thinking that colleges should set up two-year, three-year, and four-year programs (within the individual institution) to meet the needs of students who do not wish to complete four years of education or who want to compress their education into three years.

There is also recognized the need of the mature woman to add to her education and thereby to become equipped to participate more fully in her society when her childrearing duties are over. These women are needed by the community and by the nation and, since a high percentage of them will return to work or go to work for the first time, their contributions to the labor force can be heightened by additional education in their later years.

There are many other trends, needs, and pet theories about education that will continue to develop, and whether any of these will turn into reality is, of course, yet to be seen. But it is apparent that many of the changes that will come about in higher education will center on the higher education of women, for educated women are one of our most precious resources, and we must not only maintain them, we must cultivate them.

Support for Women's Education. One of the most serious needs of the higher education of women is greater financial aid. At present, women's colleges are receiving disproportionately little of the money available for the support of higher education in general.

A number of reasons are advanced for the laxity of corporate giving:

contributions to associations and to coeducational colleges, "prejudice" not so much *against* women's colleges as *for* other types of institutions, failure to realize the growing number of professional women workers, etc. But the most significant reason seems to be that, until very recently, women's colleges were not presenting their needs and stories in a convincing manner. Many were not even attempting to present a case at all. It appears that with the isolation of this factor, the women's colleges are beginning to make both joint and individual efforts to tell their story to corporations and to solici' and receive the needed support.

It is also recognized that colleges must cultivate their alumnæ more assiduously. Women are seldom in a position to provide any sizeable financial support until twenty or thirty years after graduation, and by that time many colleges have often lost track of many of them. Too, women tend to contribute less to their alma maters than do their husbands, an indication that the ties of college loyalty need to be strengthened.

Fortunately, many colleges are becoming aware of these two critical areas of financial concern and are taking steps to marshal their facts, call on corporations, cultivate their alumnae, and present their case to other constituencies. They are realizing that they have no choice in the matter, that if women's colleges are to continue to serve and progress, they must have the wherewithal—and with a little more work, they'll get it.

As American colleges, especially colleges for women, look ahead to the approaching century, they will undoubtedly cling to the best of the cultural heritage, mirror the role of the educated woman in the present society, and seek to envision what the lives of the women of tomorrow will require. With such a blending are the leaders in higher education planning their educational programs.

For of one thing they are convinced: the student can no longer be realigned to fit the old pattern; the pattern must be redesigned to fit the student. But basic to this is a restatement of philosophy and objectives in the light of current and future needs. From the restatement will stem a reshaping of the curriculum, of courses of study, of methodology, of attitudes toward students, together with a realization that this blueprint must be constantly evaluated in the light of changing conditions.

The next forty years will find women with an even greater degree of responsibility because of the increasing need for reliance on their leadership and education. Women of today and tomorrow are destined to witness their finest hour in the history of mankind. It is in helping prepare them for this hour that the colleges of America will realize one of their finest achievements.

REFERENCES

CHAPTER 1

1. Mabel Newcomer, *A Century of Higher Education For American Women* (New York: Harper and Brothers, 1959), p. 7.

2. Eleanor Flexner, *Century of Struggle* (Cambridge, Massachusetts: Harvard University Press, 1959).

3. National Manpower Council, *Womanpower* (New York: Columbia University Press, 1957), p. 9 ff.

4. David Riesman, *Some Continuities and Discontinuities in the Education of Women*, Third John Dewey Memorial Lecture (Bennington College, Bennington, Vermont, 1957).

5. Nevitt Sanford, *Our Students Today: Individualists or Conformers?*, An address given before the 31st Annual Meeting of the New York State Deans and Guidance Personnel, Elmira, New York, November 8, 1957, Mimeographed, p. 9.

6. Ernest Havemann and Patricia Salter West, *They Went To College* (New York: Harcourt Brace, 1952), pp. 27-29.

7. Robert M. Hutchins, *No Friendly Voice* (Chicago: University of Chicago Press, 1936).

8. Kate Hevner Mueller, "The Cultural Pressures of Women," *The Education of Women—Signs for the Future*, ed. Opal D. David (Washington: American Council on Education, 1959), p. 54.

9. Margaret Habein, "The Liberal Arts Program," *Ibid.*, p. 98.

10. Lloyd Warner and James Abegglen, *Big Business Leaders in America* (New York: Harper and Brothers, 1955).

CHAPTER 2

1. Harold H. Titus, *Living Issues in Philosophy* (New York: American Book Company, 1946), p. 14.

2. Walter Lippmann, "The State of Education in This Troubled World," *Vital Speeches of the Day*, II, pp. 200-203.

3. Alfred North Whitehead, *The Aims of Education* (Macmillan Company, 1929), p. 97.

CHAPTER 3

1. Robert L. Sutherland, "Some Basic Facts," *The Education of Women—Signs for the Future*, ed. Opal D. David (Washington: American Council on Education, 1959), p. 15.

CHAPTER 4

1. John Brown, "With Brains, Sir," *McGuffey's Sixth Eclectic Reader,* revised ed., January, 1880.
2. Blaise Pascal, *La Pensées,* Article II, Section 10.
3. Francis Bacon, *Novum Organum,* Section 33-44.
4. William Shakespeare, *Julius Caesar,* Act I, Section 2, i.e. 140-141.
5. James Joyce, *A Portrait of the Artist as a Young Man* (New York: Viking Press, 1956).
6. Sean O'Casey, *Within The Gates* (New York: Macmillan Company, 1934).
7. Titus Petronius Arbiter, *Satyricon,* 29:118.

CHAPTER 5

1. Elizabeth Eckhardt May and Susan Pike Corcoran, "Freshmen Interview 'Working Wives'," *Journal of Home Economics,* LI, No. 6 (June, 1959), 464-466.
2. Robert G. Foster and Pauline Park Wilson, *Women After College* (New York: Columbia University Press, 1942), pp. 227-228.
3. George D. Stoddard, *On the Education of Women* (New York: The Macmillan Co., 1950), p. 89.
4. C. S. Elvehjem, "From the Minds of Men to the Lives of People," *Journal of Home Economics,* XLIX, No. 9 (September, 1957), p. 507.
5. Nathaniel Champlin and Francis Villemain (ed.), "Dewey and Creative Education," *The Saturday Review,* November 21, 1959, p. 21.
6. *Proceedings of Conference on Values and Decision-Making in Home Management,* Michigan State University, E. Lansing, July 4-6, 1955.
7. National Manpower Council, *Work in the Lives of Married Women* (New York: Columbia University Press, 1958), p. 220.
8. Gertrude Chittenden and Flo Gould, "A Challenge to Child Development and Family Relations, 1959," *Journal of Home Economics,* LI, No. 2 (February, 1959), pp. 97-99.
9. John E. Anderson, "The Development of Behavior and Personality," Vol. 2: Development and Education, *The Nation's Children,* Eli Ginzberg, editor, *The 1960 White House Conference on Children and Youth* (New York: Columbia University Press, 1960).
10. Ernst W. Burgess and Paul Wallin, *Engagement and Marriage* (New York: J. B. Lippincott Company, 1953), p.v.
11. *Ibid.,* p. 1.
12. James G. Miller, Director, Mental Health Research Institute. Mimeographed copy of talk on "What the Public Doesn't Know About Behavioral Sciences—and Should," given in the Thomas Alva Edison Conference on "The Mass Media and the Image of Science," Washington, D. C., November 6, 1959.
13. Harold P. Halpert, "Activities of the National Institute of Mental Health Which Affect American Families," *Marriage and Family Living, Journal of National Council on Family Relations,* August, 1958, pp. 261-269.

CHAPTER 7

1. Talcott Parsons and Robert F. Bales, *Family, Socialization and Interaction Process* (Glencoe, Illinois: The Free Press, 1955).
2. Abraham Maslow, *Motivation and Personality* (New York: Harper & Brothers, 1954).

CHAPTER 8

1. David Riesman, *The Lonely Crowd* (New Haven: Yale University Press, 1950).
2. Marie Jahoda and Joan Havel, "Psychological Problems of Women in Different Social Roles," *The Educational Record*, XXXVI, No. 4 (Washington: American Council on Education, 1955).
3. William H. Whyte, *The Organization Man* (New York: Simon and Schuster, 1956).
4. Margaret Mead, *Male and Female* (New York: W. Morrow, 1949).

CHAPTER 10

1. Leo C. Muller and Ouida Gean Muller, *College for Coeds* (New York: Pitman Publishing Corporation, 1960).
2. *The Great Heritage*, A brochure by the Development Committee, Saint Mary's College, Notre Dame, Indiana.
3. G. K. Hodenfield, Associated Press education release, January 14, 1960.
4. Anne W. Langman, "Why are College Presidents Resigning?" *McCall's*, May 1959, p. 138.
5. "Corporate Support of Women's Colleges: A Survey of Corporation Attitudes," A research progress report produced jointly by The Dumore Foundation (Racine, Wisconsin), Saint Mary's College (Notre Dame, Indiana), and John Price Jones Company, Inc. (New York), pp. 2-3.
6. Otto F. Kraushaar, "Industrial Support for the Women's Colleges," *Bulletin of Association of American Colleges*, March 1956.
7. "Corporate Support of Women's Colleges: A Survey of Corporation Attitudes," *op. cit.*
8. "Affectionately . . . , " *Time*, May 2, 1960, p. 42.
9. Gordon W. Blackwell, "To Educate A Woman Costs More," *Woman's College News*, XLVIII, No. 7 (Greensboro: University of North Carolina, April 1959).
10. Letter to editors from Sister Mary Rhodes of Loretto Heights College, Loretto, Colorado, April 1960.
11. Dexter M. Keezer (ed.), *Financing Higher Education—1960-70* (New York: McGraw-Hill Book Company, Inc., 1959), p. 1.
12. Richard Glenn Gettell, "A Plea for the Uncommon Woman," Inaugural address delivered at Mount Holyoke College, South Hadley, Massachusetts, November 9, 1957.

13. Harvie Branscomb, "Mutuality of Business and Education," An address given at the Birmingham-Southern College Industry Conference, 1958.

14. William R. Cole, III, "In the College Troubled Times . . . " *Commonwealth, The Magazine of Virginia* (Richmond: Virginia State Chamber of Commerce, December 1957).

15. From an address by Carter Davidson, President of Union College, at a Conference on Industry and the Liberal Arts, Corning, New York, October, 1953.

16. Frank A. Sparks, An address given at the Workshop On Planning and Development in Higher Education, Indiana University, July 23-August 7, 1959 (Mimeographed).

17. Rembrandt C. Hiller, Jr., "The Why and Wherefore of Company Contributions," *The Bulletin,* V (The American Association of Fund-Raising Counsel, August 3, 1959).

18. Letter from Francis C. Pray, Vice-President—College Relations, Council for Financial Aid to Education, Inc., New York, April 14, 1960.